CAREERS

Exploration and Decision
Second Edition

Jack L. Rettig
Oregon State University
College of Business

Fearon Education
a division of
David S. Lake Publishers
Belmont, California

For June, Rick, and Mico

Illustrator: Elizabeth Callen

Copyright © 1986 by David S. Lake Publishers, 19 Davis Drive,
Belmont, California 94002. All rights reserved. No part of this
book may be reproduced by any means, transmitted, or translated
into a machine language without written permission from the
publisher.

ISBN-0-8224-4679-0

Library of Congress Catalog Card Number: 85-50617
Printed in the United States of America

2. 9 8 7 6 5 4 3

7154738

Contents

Preface

This book is for you and for every other young person faced with the problem of choosing a career. It contains ideas and information that will help you make the best possible career choice.

The book begins by explaining the reasons that people enter the occupations they do. It then helps you explore both yourself and the world of work. The process of making a career decision is explained, and you are shown how to compare and evaluate occupations. The final chapters prepare you to enter your career by offering specific advice for finding a job and making a living.

While writing this book, I have been helped by many people. Some are mentioned in the book, but the great majority must remain anonymous. They know who they are, and I am grateful to each one. Two of my colleagues at Oregon State University, however, deserve a special note of thanks. They are Professors Louis Edwards and Robert McCain. Each, in his own way, made this a better book. Mary Lorenz of David S. Lake Publishers provided outstanding editorial assistance.

To you, the reader, I send every good wish for a lifetime of fulfillment in this complex and difficult world. Without that wish for your future, this book would not exist at all.

J.L.R.

How People Choose Their Occupations

Some Expert Opinions

Dreams cost nothing
unless you want them to come true.

"Rich man, poor man, beggar man, thief. Doctor, lawyer, merchant chief." We used to chant that jingle when I was a kid. There were more words to it, I think. And maybe it went with a game. I can't remember. But I do remember how we used to talk and dream about what we'd be when we grew up.

How the years have flown! Some of our dreams have become realities. Joe is a mechanic. Mary teaches school. Pam is a buyer in a store downtown. Bob Wilson is a doctor. And Bill—well, Bill just takes what he can get.

How did it happen? Every person has a story. Ask a dozen people how they chose their careers and you'll get a dozen different answers. One followed in his father's footsteps. One just drifted into something. One got pushed. Another discovered an occupation that "turned her on." One had to take what was available at the time and "just sort of stayed with it." Everybody ends up somewhere.

Do you have any control over where you end up? Can you really choose your own road, follow it, and end up at a chosen destination? Well, maybe not entirely. Too many unexpected things happen. Still, most people do have some control. If they want something, plan for it, strive for it, and get a few breaks, the chances are they can get where they want to go.

To get into the proper occupation, you must know yourself. You must know occupations. And you must be able to match your talents with an occupation. This takes time and effort. It

1

also takes good sense. You have all of these. You CAN make a good occupational choice.

It's amazing, though, how many people make poor career choices. One expert has said that 80% of the working people in America are in the wrong jobs. He didn't mean that all those folks had made terrible career choices. He simply meant that they could have made better ones.

An underpaid mechanic may have the ability to be an engineer. An office worker might be much happier as a landscape designer. A salesclerk in a department store may be more at home working in a lab. A firefighter may secretly wish to be a soccer coach. The world seems full of such people. They get by, but their lives are less than they might be. How do these people get into such predicaments?

It's worth thinking about. It's worth doing something about. Would you rather be one of the 20% who are in the right jobs? Or one of the 80% who could have done better? Certainly you want to be in that 20%. Then today—right now—is the time to begin doing the things that will put you there.

If you're disadvantaged and laboring under handicaps, don't give up. Keep trying. More and more people are concerned about your problems. The future certainly looks better than the past. Read on—there's good news for you.

Let's begin by looking at how people actually choose their occupations—according to the experts.

What the Experts Say

Have you ever noticed that experts don't always agree? Doctors, coaches, plumbers, and chefs often disagree with others in their fields. Experts of all kinds disagree with each other from time to time. This has happened among the experts on occupational choice as well.

There are a number of reasons for these disagreements. The experts' methods differ. Their assumptions differ, and their goals differ. They work with different people, at different times and places. But the main trouble is that research on human beings is hard to do. People are complex. They keep changing while they are being studied.

So the experts have come up with different answers to the question, "How do people choose their occupations?" Here are some of their theories. While the theories vary, there is value in every one.

Early Childhood Influences One theory[1] says that adults tend to seek work in situations like those they had enjoyed as children. They also try to avoid work situations that remind them of painful childhood experiences. Thus a person who grew up in a warm, accepting family might choose a "person-directed" career. Such jobs require one to work a lot with other people. Good examples would be teaching, sales, or social work.

A person who grew up in a cold, rejecting family would be inclined to choose a "non-person-directed" career. Such careers —like astronomy, accounting, or engineering—don't often require much contact with people.

This theory about early childhood influences is difficult to prove. A lot of things can happen over the years. Some of these things tend to cancel a person's childhood experiences. Even so, this theory offers ideas that we should keep in mind.

The Self-Concept Factor Another theory[2] suggests that the main factor determining one's occupational choice is self-concept. *Self-concept* can be defined as "the person you think you are." According to this theory, your self-concept develops as you grow up. Your eventual choice of a career is based on the kind of person you believe yourself to be.

Let's follow this notion for a bit. If you consider yourself to be physically strong and the outdoors type, you might be inclined to choose a tough, rugged occupation. You might want to be a logger, a heavy equipment operator, or an oil field roustabout. If you think you are clever and a good talker, you might choose to be a salesperson. If you think you are artistic and creative, you might choose to become a designer or commercial artist. The whole idea is that you choose your career according to the kind of person you think you are.

Many people agree with this idea. Some, however, think the idea doesn't go far enough. The critics think that one's career choice is affected by many things in addition to self-concept. For example, they believe that career choice is affected by family pressures and the geographical area in which a person grows up. Career choice also might be affected by the quality of the schools attended and the income level of the family. A person's knowledge of careers, the jobs that actually are available, how ambitious or lazy a person is, and so forth, might be other career-choice factors.

Personality A third theory[3] suggests that choosing an occupation is just a way of expressing one's personality. This theory says that people who go into a specific career tend to have similar personalities. Therefore, making a good career choice means matching your personality with a career that suits it.

This theory holds that there are six basic personality types. These are the types: Realistic, Intellectual, Social, Conventional, Enterprising, and Artistic. It is said that all occupations can be put into six groups with these same names. So if a person with a Realistic personality chooses a Realistic career, everything should work out fine. The theory is really a bit more complex than that, but this is the basic idea. In Chapter 4, this theory will be more fully explained.

Chance Quite a few people seem to believe that a person sometimes enters a career because of things that "just happen." This is the element of chance.

A good example of chance is given in this story. A young college student was studying to become an engineer. On a Christmas vacation, he had a skiing accident and broke his leg. While in the hospital, he became friendly with the doctor. One thing led to another, and the end result was that this young man decided to change his whole career plan. He went back to school, dropped engineering, and shifted to the study of medicine. He is an M.D. today, but feels sure that he would be an engineer if he had not had that accident.

His experience was dramatic, but it doesn't have to be that way. Another example is that of a young woman in high school. She decided to become a journalist after getting into a conversation with a reporter on a train. A third example is that of a young man who decided he wanted to manage a garden shop after working in a nursery during a summer vacation. His whole life was changed because he answered a help-wanted ad in a newspaper.

A Slow, Complicated Process   Another group of experts wrote a book on occupational choice[4] that has had a lot of influence. Their theory has three parts:

1. Occupational choice is a process that takes place over a period of eight or ten years, roughly between the ages of ten and twenty.
2. During this time, a young person makes a series of decisions that gradually reduce the number of choices that are left.
3. Every occupational choice ends up being a compromise.

This theory is more complex than the others we have considered. It states that people's occupational choices are influenced both by things inside them (like personality and interests) and by things outside them (like family, school, things that just happen, and so on).

According to this theory, a person goes through three different periods before arriving at a career choice. The timing of all the periods, of course, varies from person to person.

The first is a "fantasy" period. It occurs roughly between the ages of 10 and 12. At this time, the young person really doesn't know very much about occupations or even about his or her abilities. Youngsters believe they can be anything they want to be. Often their imaginations run wild. They want to be astronauts, cowhands, movie stars, or baseball players. Anything is possible in this time of make-believe.

The second is called the "tentative" period. It runs approximately between the ages of 12 and 17. During this period, young people are becoming aware of their true interests and abilities. As adolescents they learn about the world of work. They discover that soon they must make their choices. They also know that they need more information before good choices can be made. These are the years of searching, reaching out, trying new things, getting acquainted with themselves and the world. In addition to asking, "What would I like to be?" they now are asking, "What am I best suited for?"

The third period is called the "realistic" period. It runs roughly between the ages of 17 and 20. During the realistic period, people know their interests and abilities pretty well. They are quite concerned with knowing the facts about the world. They know that they may have to compromise between what they would like and what is possible. They know, too, that it is time to make decisions and that there is no going back.

This matter of not being able to go back is worth thinking about. These experts believe that a person in school comes to a number of important decision points. A student taking one course will end up on a certain track. Another course will mean a different track. Dropping a course may mean being thrown off a track.

Once a person is on a track, commitments tend to build up and choices tend to narrow down. Pretty soon going back means making painful or even impossible sacrifices. High school decisions can be very important, even though they may not seem important at the time. A person's life can be affected by high school decisions that were made impulsively, accidentally, or even mistakenly.

Which Theory Is Best?

You may answer that question if you wish, but it really need not be answered. All the theories have value. All of them help us understand what is happening. Yet none of them may be completely true. If any of them were "the truth, the whole truth, and nothing but the truth," we wouldn't call it a theory. We would call it a "law." A theory is a belief, not a proven fact.

So we don't have all the answers when it comes to understanding occupational choice. A lot of smart people have worked very hard to discover the answers that we have. We should be grateful to all of them. So let's not ask which theory is best. Instead, let's use what we can from each of them.

If you want to read more about these and other theories, see the Bibliography in the back of this book. Then look up the reference materials in your school or public library. Quite a lot of information is available.

One Final Point

The things you've read so far may lead you to think that the career-choice process ends when you take your first full-time job. That's not true. The process of searching and matching goes on throughout life. Some people change careers several times. Our main concern in this book, though, is with your first occupational decision. If that is a good one, you won't flounder so much later on.

Beginning in Chapter 5, we'll talk about the meaning of work and what happens during a person's working life. We'll talk about getting a job, and what it's like to work for a living. We'll also talk about job changes in mid-career.

In the next few chapters, we're going to talk about *you*. We're going to ask a pretty big question: "Who are you?" This may sound like an easy question. Actually, it's a very difficult one to answer. We won't be able to answer it completely. Still, the ideas we'll consider should help as you explore the fascinating question of who you really are.

QUESTIONS FOR THOUGHT AND DISCUSSION

1. At what age should a person begin to think seriously about making a career choice? Why?

2. How important to one's happiness is one's occupational choice?

3. Why do we have more than one theory of occupational choice?

4. What can you think of that affects a person's career choice, but that was not included in any of our theories?

5. Why do people sometimes change occupations several times during their lives? Is changing occupations a good thing? Why or why not?

6. It is said that everything has its price. What is the price of a poor occupational choice? What are the benefits of a good one?

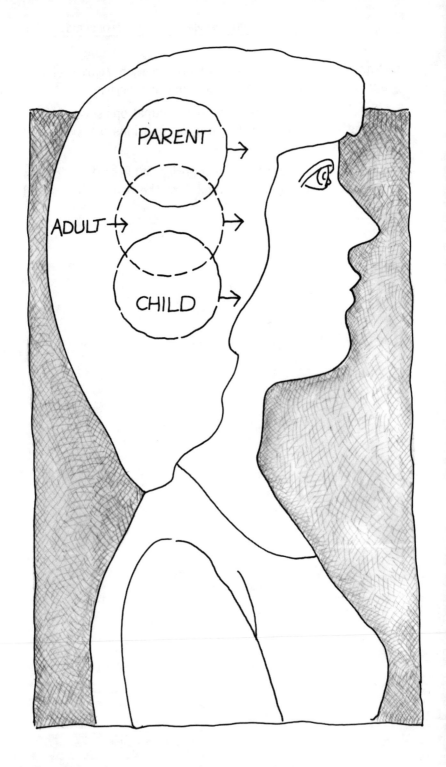

Who Are You?

Parent, Child, and Adult

The happiness of one who seeks applause is placed in the hands of others.

Who are you? You can answer in many ways. We all have a general idea of who we are. We have a name, a family, a history. We live somewhere. People know us. We think and do certain things. We've been told, "You are what you think," or "You are what you do." So each of us does have an identity, some kind of self-concept.

Yet how completely do we know ourselves? Who really knows all there is to know about "the person inside"? Most of us never fully discover who we are. Deep down inside, each of us is something of a mystery.

For many years, psychologists have been trying to solve the mystery. They've made progress, but even today few of them would claim to have the final answers. Still, they have many important things to tell us. In this book, we can't discuss all of their ideas. We will, however, discuss a few that will be especially helpful to you.

Parent, Child, and Adult

A few years ago, a book was published[1] that helped many people understand themselves a little better. This best-seller suggested that each of us is not just one person, but three.

Think about that for a minute. Each of us is three different people. We don't have three bodies, but we do have three states of being. We have three different states of mind. One is called

11

the "Parent," another is called the "Child," and the third is called the "Adult."

Each of these states of being takes over from time to time. Sometimes the Parent is in charge. Sometimes the Child takes over. Sometimes the Adult is in command. Sometimes we can control the being in charge, but sometimes we cannot. This is true for everyone. How does this work?

The Parent   According to this theory, the Parent is a large collection of "recordings." The collection is stored in a person's brain. These recordings were made during the first five years of the person's life. They contain a record of everything the little person heard or saw. Almost all of them can be recalled under the proper conditions.

The collection of recordings has one especially important part. That part is the set of rules and laws that was imposed by the young person's parents. These rules and laws helped shape the young person's beliefs. And as the child had no way to judge them, these rules and laws were recorded in his or her brain as "truth."

What do these rules and laws say? Well, that depends upon what the parents said and did. Some common rules might be: "Be kind." "Be careful." "Don't lie." "Don't steal." "Mother loves you." "Father is wise." "Work is good." Such rules help socialize and comfort a child.

However, some of the other rules might be upsetting, demeaning, or misleading. "Do it this way." "Don't do it that way." "You're bad." "You're stupid." "You're mean." "You're ridiculous." "Never give a sucker an even break." Such statements and rules can damage a person.

Every person's Parent recording is different. Each of us had a unique childhood. This theory simply suggests two things: (1) each of us has a Parent recording in our brain, and (2) this recording sometimes "comes on" and tells us what to do. It's a voice from the past, telling us what to do today.

This may give us problems. First, the information or rules in our Parent may be incorrect or out of date. Second, our

Parent sometimes can influence us without our being aware of it. When that happens, we may do things or make decisions without fully considering more correct or current data.

As you work toward choosing your career, you may be sure that your Parent will get into the act. You really can't prevent this—in fact, you might not want to. The point is that you should be aware that this Parent is influencing you. Try to take advantage of its good advice, but also try to avoid being hurt by the bad.

The Child   Each of us also has a Child inside. The Child is another set of brain recordings from the past. It, too, was made before we were five. Our Parent knows what happened outside us while we were young. The Child knows what happened inside us. The Child is a huge collection of childish feelings and emotions. They also influence us occasionally.

These are the feelings and emotions of a little person who is helpless. Children are completely dependent on others. They often are frustrated, unable to master the world around them. The very young can't even speak. Although they learn words as they get older, they still can't do many things they would like to do and that they see other people doing.

So every time a child compares himself or herself with older people, there is a feeling of being inadequate. The child can't run as fast, jump as high, or throw as far. The child is little, weak, and can't even tie shoelaces. As a result, the child begins to feel Not OK. This feeling of being Not OK is permanently recorded in the Child.

According to the theory, every one of us has a Not OK Child inside. When it asserts itself, we feel inferior.

How does this tie in with choosing an occupation? It means that a person should be very careful not to let the Child's feelings of inferiority stand in the way of making an intelligent career choice.

Many of us impose unnecessary limitations upon ourselves. We say, or think, we can't do something without really checking. We hold ourselves back when we could move ahead. We assume that certain good careers are closed to us when they are really not closed at all. We think we're Not OK when we're really just as good as the next person. When that happens, it's often the work of our Child. We shouldn't let it happen.

This theory has a lot more to say about the Child. However, if you really understand just that one idea of not letting your Child inhibit you in choosing a career, the theory has served you well.

The Adult   The Adult is the third state of being that exists inside us. Our Adult is very different from our Parent and our Child. Our Adult lives in the present. The other two states of being live in the past. The Adult is more like a computer than a recording. It helps us to control our other states of being.

The Adult begins to develop in us at the age of about ten months. This is when we are first able to move around and do things on our own. As soon as we start becoming independent people, our Adult begins to develop. At first the Adult is very weak. But by the time a person is 12, the Adult is able to work fairly well.

The Adult is the logical, rational part of a person's thinking process. It helps us to see and understand what's happening in the real world here and now. It allows us to make realistic predictions about the future. Actually, the Adult receives information from three sources: from the Parent, from the Child, and from the outside world. The Adult then compares these inputs and analyzes for itself.

Things work out well as long as the Adult can give the proper weight to inputs from the outside world. But this doesn't always happen. Sometimes the input flowing from the Parent is too strong. Then the Parent takes over, and the person follows instructions from the past. Sometimes the input from the Child is too strong. Then the person gets careless or afraid. So the Adult isn't always in control. Sometimes a person's three states of being seem to argue among themselves. Then the person is really confused.

Signals coming in from the outside world register on all three of a person's states of being. All three are always there, ready to take over. In a given situation, which one will gain control? Let's consider an example.

An Example

A young woman parks her shiny new car in a parking lot. As she's walking away, a young man wheels into the adjacent slot. As he pulls in, he creases the first car's fender. All three of the young woman's states of being—Parent, Child, and Adult—saw what happened. The Parent (who may believe in "an eye for an eye") says, "I'll sue him!" The Child (I'm Not OK) says, "Maybe I parked over the line." The Adult says, "Let's keep calm and figure out the best way to deal with this."

Well, who will win? It depends. It depends upon the strengths of the young woman's Parent, Child, and Adult at that particular time. It depends on what the other person does. It depends on how things have gone for the young woman that day. It depends on a lot of things. But most would agree that it would be best if the Adult took over. At the same time, we probably can see how all three states of being would be tugging on us in that situation.

Of course, not every Parent believes in "an eye for an eye." Another young person's Parent might say, "Turn the other cheek." In that case the young person might be concerned about damage to the other driver's car. The point is not so much what the Parent says. Rather, the point is that there does seem to be a Parent in all of us—and that Parent is a voice from the past, telling us what to do.

Who Will Decide for You?

It is fortunate when a person finds that much of the information in his or her Parent is in line with today's real world. The information from this person's Parent is reliable. It is not always telling the person not to believe what he or she sees. It is not telling the person not to do what seems proper at the time. Such a Parent is not continually holding a person back.

Some people may have a lot of conflict between the Parent and the Adult. These people may find it hard to develop a philosophy to live by. Take the example of a youngster whose father was a drunk and whose mother stole for a living. This youngster probably has a loud recording in the Parent that says, "Never trust a cop."

Yet one day this person may meet a friendly police officer who speaks in a quiet voice and is helpful. The Parent says one thing, but the Adult says another. Which can be believed? This kind of thing may happen over and over, with the Parent saying "No" and the Adult saying "Yes." Then what is going to happen to this person's beliefs about the world?

None of us ever escapes our Child completely, either. In one way, our Child is a blessing. It is open, free, and willing to try new things. But at the same time the Child thinks it is Not OK. The Not OK Child constantly tries to hold the Adult back. This conflict tends to confuse us. Yet all of us encounter this conflict from time to time. Our task is to keep it under control.

There are several reasons for mentioning these ideas. First, it is important to understand the effect our Parent and our Child can have on our decisions. These old brain recordings can have a strong influence on us, even though they may not contain up-to-date information. In Chapter 1, we discussed the possible influences of childhood experiences on occupational choice. Now the idea is cropping up again in a somewhat different way. Many psychologists believe that the effects of our childhoods stay with us up to and long after the time when we must choose our occupations. We cannot escape these influences, but we can try to understand them. We can try to make sure that they carry no more weight than they should.

Second, choosing your occupation is such an important matter that you really should know about your Adult. If this theory is right and you do have a Parent, a Child, and an Adult, which of them should choose your occupation? It's so easy to sit back and let your Parent or your Child make the decision. But is this really the way you want to go? That question deserves some thought.

QUESTIONS FOR THOUGHT AND DISCUSSION

1. Think of someone you know. Describe an incident in which that person's Child took over. How could the person's behavior have been improved?

2. Think of someone you know. Describe an incident in which that person's Parent took over. Was the person helped or hindered by the Parent? Does the Parent usually help, or hinder? Or is there a pattern? Why do you think so?

3. Think of an experience you have had in which your Adult took over. How do you feel about that experience? Why?

4. Which do you prefer to have in command—your Parent, your Child, or your Adult? Why?

5. To what extent can you control whether your Parent, Child, or Adult is in command? How do you exercise this control?

6. It has been said that a good theory is the most practical thing in the world. What does that statement mean?

Who Are You?

Human Needs

*Our needs determine us more than
we determine them.*

In addition to knowing about our states of being, it also is helpful to understand why we do the things we do. Why is it that the Parent "comes on" sometimes? Why does our Child sometimes take over? Why isn't our Adult always in command? Why do we go to school? Why do we work? Why do we do anything?

To answer such questions, we turn now to a well-established explanation of human behavior. This theory says that motivation is based on inner needs.[1] (There are other explanations of human behavior, but for now the need theory will serve us best.) To put it simply, this theory suggests that everything we do is done for a purpose. That purpose, whether we realize it or not, is to satisfy our inner needs.

Think about that for a minute. This theory says that everything we do—everything—is done to satisfy some need that we have. We spend our entire lives—working, playing, studying, eating, you name it—trying to satisfy our needs. If this is true, and if we truly understand our needs, then we can truly understand our behavior. We also can make very intelligent occupational choices. Let's take a look at this theory.

Needs and Wants

To begin, we should understand the difference between a need and a want. A "want" is a conscious desire for something. If you have a want, you know it. It may be a want for a vacation trip, a new pair of shoes, a date with so-and-so, or simply a bite to eat. You always are consciously aware of your wants.

A "need" is something different. A need is a basic human requirement. However, a person may or may not know that it exists. In other words, while a want always is conscious, a need may be conscious or unconscious. If you need a drink of water you are likely to know it. But what if you need to make up a vitamin deficiency, or need recognition from someone? You may be consciously aware of those things. If this theory is right, you will be motivated (driven from the inside) by your need, whether you are aware of it or not.

Five Basic Needs

If people work to meet their needs, it would be good to know what these needs are. They are very simple. This theory suggests that people have only five needs. Everyone has them, and all of us spend our lives trying to satisfy them. Although we may try to satisfy our needs in different ways, we all are trying to satisfy the same needs. In a way, it is these needs— common to all people—that make us human. They seem to be a basic part of human nature.

The needs are said to occur in the order shown below. They can briefly be described as follows:

1. *The Physiological Needs.* Our needs for the things that keep our bodies alive—food, water, air, rest, elimination, and so forth. These needs come first. We must meet them, or we will die.
2. *The Safety Needs.* First we need to stay alive, and then we need to be safe. There are two kinds of safety needs: the need to be physically safe and the need to be psychologically safe or secure.
3. *The Belongingness Needs.* Once we are alive and safe, we then try to satisfy our social needs. There is a need

to be with and accepted by other people. And we discover our need for love.

4. *The Esteem Needs.* After our first three needs are fairly well met, we try to satisfy a fourth need. We look for recognition, respect, reputation. There are two forms of this need: self-esteem (thinking well of ourselves) and the esteem of others.

5. *The Self-Actualization Needs.* Our highest need is to actualize ourselves, to achieve our full potential, to become all that we might be. This need is one that no one ever satisfies completely. In part, this is because we are too busy trying to satisfy our lower needs.

If the need theory is correct, those are the things we are after. Our work, rest, play—whatever we do—is done in an effort to meet one or more of those needs.

Some activities are more rewarding than others in helping us meet our needs. The wise person will try to spend his or her time doing those things that are most rewarding. That's one reason why it's so important to make a good occupational choice. If you make a poor occupational choice, you will have to do a lot of things that really are not satisfying. And in the end, your total life will be less rewarding than it might have been. Despite your efforts, some of your important needs will not have been well met.

The Need Pyramid

There are some other things we have to say about this theory. We have said that human needs seem to occur in a certain order. A good way to visualize the order in which our needs occur is to think of a pyramid, as shown in Figure 1 on page 22.

You are always trying to climb the pyramid. You have to climb over the first step before you can get to the second. You must pass the second before you reach the third, and so on. During a day or a week, things happen that tend to push you

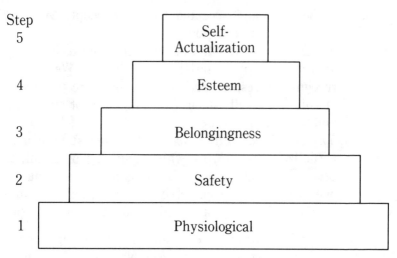

Step
5

4

3

2

1

Figure 1 **The Need Pyramid**

up or down the pyramid. But you are always trying to climb as high as possible.

Let's look at an example of people moving up and down the pyramid. Suppose that two friends are riding home from school on their bikes. It's a Friday afternoon. They're laughing, horsing around, and talking about tonight's game. They're probably somewhere in the middle of the pyramid, trying to satisfy their needs for belongingness and esteem.

Suddenly a truck roars around the corner at high speed and heads straight for them. What happens? Well, it is likely that they will forget all about belongingness and esteem and start thinking about safety in a hurry. Their safety needs are threatened, and they act accordingly. They slide down the pyramid.

Let's give the story a happy ending and say that they escape the danger. What happens then? After they stop shaking, they will put their safety needs behind them. Once again they will move up the pyramid to belongingness and esteem. Later, they may even add a few details to the story to get a little extra esteem from their friends.

Each of us moves up and down our need pyramid every day. These movements usually are not dramatic, but we move just the same. We move down the pyramid each time we get hungry or tired. We move up each time we try to impress somebody. But throughout the day our basic drive is always to climb as high as we can.

Unsatisfied Needs Make Us "Go"

What drives or motivates a person at any given time? Many experts believe that at any given time, any given person is being motivated by his or her lowest unsatisfied need. That's an important point: at any given time, any given person is being motivated by his or her lowest unsatisfied need.

The point is not hard to see. Let's oversimplify just a little. We can say that a person works on a need until that need is reasonably well satisfied. The person then moves on to the next need. He or she works on that need until it is reasonably

well satisfied and then moves on to a third one. As soon as any need is satisfied, it is left behind. The person moves on to the next unsatisfied need. As long as a need is satisfied, it does not push or drive a person. It's still there, but it is inactive.

For example, consider your need for food. After a big meal, you are full. You still have a need for food, and soon it will motivate you again. But for the moment your need for food is satisfied. As long as your food need is satisfied, your body will not push you to eat any more.

Satisfied needs do not motivate. Only unsatisfied needs motivate. And the lowest unsatisfied need on a person's pyramid is the one that motivates him or her at any given time. Why? Because the needs below that level are satisfied and therefore inactive, and because the needs at the higher levels have not yet been reached.

Your lower needs are very powerful. Whenever a low-level need becomes unsatisfied, it will pull you down to that level. This happens no matter how high up the pyramid you may have been. Let's take a really wild example to show how this works.

Suppose you're in a classroom. It's a basement room with no windows. Class is going on as usual, and you're probably trying to satisfy your needs for belongingness and esteem. Now suppose there's a maniac outside the room. He quietly locks the doors and seals up the room so it is airtight.

He drills a six-inch hole near the bottom of one wall, and another six-inch hole in the ceiling. Then he hooks up a fire hose to the hole in the wall and starts filling the room with water. As water comes in one hole, air goes out the other. You're locked in and you can't get out. The water rushes in, and it's quickly up to your ankles. Then it's up to your hips, and to your shoulders. Pretty soon you're swimming around for dear life.

Only a few minutes ago you had been motivated by your needs for belongingness and esteem. But what's motivating you now? It's the sheer need to survive.

The water keeps getting higher and higher, and pretty soon it's almost to the ceiling. Some of your friends have drowned. The rest of you are fighting to stay alive. How likely is it that one person would say to another, "You go ahead and breathe—I'll drown first"?

The need to survive will take over. Almost anyone in that room would try to get that last breath of air before the room is completely filled with water.

Well, that's a cruel and unlikely story. But it does show how people might act under extreme conditions. Those low-level needs are very strong in most people. They often are much more powerful than the more civilized needs at higher levels on the pyramid.

Our Needs Overlap

Now let's make the pyramid a little less rigid. Actually, our needs are not quite like the blocks in a pyramid. They don't have abrupt beginnings and endings. Instead, they gradually merge into one another. The safety needs, for example, blend into the physiological needs on one side and into the belongingness needs on the other.

Consider this situation. If you have to go into a tough part of town late at night, you are likely to ask one or more people to go with you. Why? Well, by getting some companions you satisfy your safety needs, first of all. And if you are attacked, having friends around probably would help your chances of survival. This would satisfy a basic physiological need—the need to stay alive. In addition, having company may help to satisfy your belongingness needs.

So you can see that satisfying our needs is not quite like taking abrupt steps up a ladder. Our needs are related to each other and blend together. By taking a single action, we may help to satisfy more than one need at a time. Also, it is not unusual for a person to be motivated by more than one need at a time.

For example, what motivates people to take jobs? Well, they might be trying to get food, clothing, and shelter to satisfy their physiological needs. But they also may be trying to save a little money so they can feel safe. In addition, they may be hoping for some belongingness from the people with whom they work. And if they are lucky, their jobs may help provide esteem from friends and co-workers. Finally, if their jobs are really great, they may get a chance to grow toward self-actualization, the highest need of all.

Therefore, a good job can truly help a person meet all his or her needs. Some jobs can help a person more than others. Pointing out that fact is one of the main purposes of this book.

Different People, Different Pyramids

So far, we've discovered that everyone has a pyramid. We've found that everyone has the same needs in his or her pyramid, and that everyone's needs come in the same order. What hasn't been said is that everyone has these needs in the same amount. Why? Because people *don't* have these needs in equal amounts. Different people's pyramids are constructed differently.

Because of this, the need pyramid on page 22 may be a little misleading. It shows all the need blocks being equally thick. This isn't necessarily true.

Some people develop a great need for safety. These are often people who have had difficult lives. They've found the world to be a scary place. A hermit, for example, is unwilling to mix with other people. This person may be trying to find safety in isolation.

Let's take the case of José Hermit. José is a weaver. He weaves fabric and tapestries on a hand loom. José was mugged three times in one year in the large city where he lived. He decided to become a hermit so he could get away from people and feel safe. He moved to a shack in the mountains. He eats very simple food and goes to town about once a month. There he sells a few weavings, picks up supplies, and sees his old friend Sam. While in the mountains, José has been able to concentrate on his work. He has become a real artist. His beautiful weaving work has become well known in the area.

Now let's look at José's need pyramid (Figure 2). We'll start at the bottom. José's physiological block is thinner than that on the basic need pyramid. He needs less in the way of food and shelter than another person needs. José's safety block is much thicker than the one on the basic pyramid. After all, José did leave society in order to assure his safety. His belongingness block is much thinner than that on the basic pyramid. Except for his visits to town, José does not need the company of others. His esteem block is about normal size, because José is proud that other people like his work. Finally, José's self-actualization block is thicker than the average person's. His potential as a weaver has increased a great deal while he has been in the mountains.

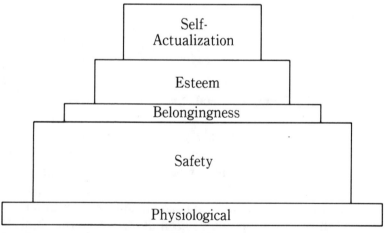

Figure 2 **José Hermit's Need Pyramid**

Now let's take a peek at Lolly Olympic's need pyramid (Figure 3). Lolly is in training for several Olympic skiing events. Her physiological block is somewhat larger than average. As an athlete in training, Lolly is especially concerned with proper food, rest, and so forth. Her safety and belongingness blocks are thinner than normal. Like many dedicated athletes, Lolly is more concerned with winning her events than with safety and belongingness. But Lolly's esteem and self-actualization blocks are quite a bit thicker than a non-competitor's. Lolly wants very badly to be recognized as a champion and to have others think well of her. And she certainly wants to achieve her full potential as a skier.

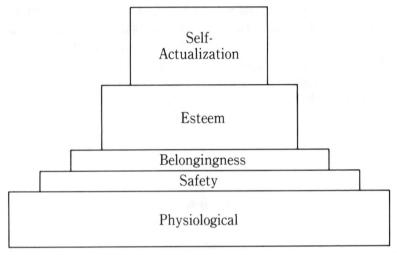

Figure 3 **Lolly Olympic's Need Pyramid**

And so it goes. A starving young artist living in an attic seems to need self-actualization at any cost. A teenager who joins every organization in town needs more belongingness than most others. A shy student is seeking safety. These people aren't crazy or even terribly abnormal. They're just different because their experiences have been different. So the point is that while everyone seems to have all five needs, not everyone has them in the same amount.

Probably you could draw your own need pyramid, showing the thicknesses of the five blocks. You then could draw another pyramid for your father, your mother, or someone else you know quite well. The chances are that the pyramids would be different, especially if there is a generation gap between the people. Why? Because different generations of people have different experiences. Many older people still have big safety needs because of the Great Depression of the 1930s. If you doubt this, ask your parents or your grandparents about it.

Where We Are

Where is the average person on the need pyramid most of the time? Many experts believe that most Americans spend much of their time at the middle levels of the pyramid. They believe that most of us are able to do a good job of meeting our physiological and safety needs. There are exceptions, of course, but generally this seems to be true. With these lower needs reasonably well satisfied, we find ourselves seeking belongingness and esteem.

Our highest need is for self-actualization, but most of us aren't able to spend very much time at that level. Most of the time we seem to be above the physiological and safety levels, but below self-actualization. We seem to be part of what has been called an "other-directed" society. We seek to belong, to be loved, and to be respected.

It's an interesting idea. Try it out on yourself. What are you really seeking most of the time? How are you going to find it in your career?

Why People Work

Let's get back to the question of why people work. We have seen that people work to satisfy their needs. We also have seen that while everyone has the same needs, not everyone's pyramid is constructed of equal-sized blocks. Fortunately, different kinds of careers make it possible for different people to satisfy differing patterns of needs.

Each person should try to find the career that best matches his or her individual pattern of needs. A person simply must do this if he or she wants the best possible life. And as we shall see later, the better a person is able to satisfy these needs right on the job, the less "work" his or her occupation will be.

About Money

By this time you may have said to yourself, "That's all very interesting. But I always thought that people worked for money." Well, you're right. People do work for money. But why do they want the money? This brings us right back to human needs. People want money because it helps them satisfy their needs. Cars and clothes, beans and bread—the things that money can buy—simply help people meet their needs.

Actually, money may be more helpful in meeting some needs than in meeting others. Take survival—the physiological needs. With money, a person can buy food, clothing, and shelter—the things required to meet those needs. There's no question about it. Money also can do a lot to help meet the safety need, especially the need for psychological safety. With a large bank account, a person may feel financially secure.

But as we move up the pyramid to the higher needs, money may begin to lose some of its effectiveness. To what extent can you buy belongingness and love? In a superficial way, these things can be bought. We've all heard of fair-weather friends. There are such people. They tend to be attracted to people with money. But belongingness and love of a more genuine and lasting kind aren't for sale. Money is not a handicap in finding belongingness and love, but you can't depend on money alone to obtain them.

Esteem—can we buy esteem with money? Well, in American society we do tend, in a general way, to give esteem to people with money. It's part of our Puritan ethic. Money and success are viewed with approval. This idea has taken a beating in recent years, but it's still with us. Probably most of us do give esteem to people with money. But the esteem that we give them may not be very deep.

Having money may bring us self-esteem, especially if we earned it. But we probably respect ourselves more for our actual accomplishments than for the money we earn. Money may not hurt our efforts to gain self-esteem, but money alone will not provide it.

Self-actualization, the highest need on our pyramid, would be the hardest of all to buy. This need calls for a person to develop skills, knowledge, and all capabilities to their limit. This takes effort more than money. But once again, money wouldn't hinder development. With money a person can buy time, or equipment, or travel. All of these things may help in the search for self-actualization. Money can't develop people, but it might help them to develop themselves.

So in answer to the question, "Don't people work for money?" we have to say, "Sure, people work for money." It's foolish to deny this fact. People work for money because it helps them satisfy their needs. When a person is on the lower levels of the pyramid, money can provide a great deal of help. As one climbs the pyramid, money may become less and less essential in meeting one's needs. Still, money is not likely to hold a person back, no matter where on the pyramid one is. The thing to remember is that there's a lot more to living than just making money.

QUESTIONS FOR THOUGHT AND DISCUSSION

1. How does a "need" differ from a "want"?

2. Give examples of three common, conscious wants that people have. Now give examples of three needs that people have, of which they may not normally be aware.

3. Explain how a person's behavior can be affected by a need of which he or she is not even aware.

4. Which is more fundamental—"wants" or "needs"? Do wants normally spring from needs, or vice versa?

5. Draw your own need pyramid. Then draw your parents' need pyramids, as you understand them. Explain the reasons for any differences.

6. Why is it important to consider the sizes of the blocks on your need pyramid as you think about possible careers?

Who Are You?

Types of Personalities

Success is caused more by attitudes than by capacities.

In the last two chapters, we've discussed our states of being and our needs. Now let's consider some types of personalities that people have. The following ideas may help you further understand who and what you are.

You will recall our brief discussion of personality types in Chapter 1. It was suggested that there are six basic kinds of personalities. These types are: Realistic, Intellectual, Social, Conventional, Enterprising, and Artistic. It also was suggested that there are certain kinds of careers that might be best for individuals with each type of personality.

A description of each personality type follows so you can get an idea of where you fit. It is quite possible that your personality pattern fits into more than one type. If so, don't let this bother you. The groups are very helpful, but lots of people can't be neatly pigeonholed. Remember too that none of these types is considered better than any other. They just try to describe people as they are.

The Realistic Type

People with realistic personalities tend to be aggressive and physically strong. They usually are not too interested in social activities. These people tend to have good physical coordination. They like to work with tools, animals, and machines.

Realistic people are not very talkative and are not very interested in being leaders. They like sports and crafts, may be good in math, but are not great readers.

Realistic people tend to be conservative in dress and manner. They think of themselves as stable, genuine, practical, and interested in the here and now. They admire people such as inventors or astronauts. A realistic young person may be thinking about going into one of the technical trades. He or she may consider becoming an equipment operator, or possibly being a forest ranger or a mechanic. It's a down-to-earth personality group.

A good example of the realistic type of person is Jim E., a forestry student in college. Jim is a big, strong guy who is not afraid of physical work. He loves nature and has a dog. He doesn't show off much, but he has been known to arm wrestle with the best. He's great with those big hands, and he knows how to fix things. If he can't fix it, he'll make a new one. He finds challenge in practical problems that have practical solutions. He talks straight and keeps his word. Jim is more willing than most to help a fellow human with a problem. In many ways people like Jim are the salt of the earth.

The Intellectual Type

The intellectuals are more interested in working with words and ideas than with physical things. They consider themselves bright, independent, thoughtful, critical, curious, persistent, self-controlled, and possibly not too sociable. They like science, art, music, reading, and foreign languages. They like to achieve in school.

Although original in ideas, intellectuals often do not make very good leaders. They believe that power comes through knowledge, rather than through an ability to command. They tend to avoid crowds and sometimes put themselves down socially. Their motor skills may not be very good. They admire people such as scientists, writers, and educators. The young intellectual may be thinking of becoming a doctor, a scientist, or a writer.

Kim P., a biology student, is a good example of the intellectual type. Kim is an excellent student. She may get so wound up in what she's saying that she forgets that many students really don't care about her subject. However, she is usually right. She likes to do extra reading and talk about it. She writes good term papers. Although she is very concerned about our society in a general way, she sometimes doesn't seem too concerned about the people around her. She wants to get an advanced degree. She hopes to make an important contribution to science.

The Social Type

As you might expect, people of the social type are very interested in other people. They are interested in student government, community service, dramatics, and public speaking. Such people often are not very interested in athletics, tools, or machines. They think well of themselves and feel that they make good leaders. They tend to be popular in school and often get good grades.

The self-image of the social type includes being cheerful, helpful, energetic, and achieving. These people may be pretty good amateur psychologists. Practical, flexible, and dependable, the social type admires such people as judges and members of Congress. Young people in this group may be thinking of becoming teachers, politicians, missionaries, or social workers.

People of this type seem to be awfully busy. Ann H., a class officer, is a good example. Ann is a very popular young woman. She works long hours, speaks up on the issues, and really gets things done. While many people of this type get good grades, Ann usually gets C's. She could get higher grades if she weren't so involved in other things. Ann sees her mission as being a mover and shaker. She helps to get things done by prodding other people into useful activity. Although she doesn't always say it, she is often disappointed when people don't measure up to her expectations.

The Conventional Type

People of the conventional type tend to be neat, sociable, and well controlled. They usually create a good first impression. They are conservative, interested in financial matters, and perhaps a little inflexible. They are not too interested in athletics or religious affairs. They usually do very well in economics, math, business, and sometimes in journalism.

Conventional people see themselves as shrewd, practical, hardheaded, and hardworking. They are precise and careful about details. They like to solve problems and to sort things out. They rate themselves low on leadership but high on dependability and perseverance. Their heroes might include well-known financiers or business leaders. They may want to become accountants, office managers, or efficiency experts.

Don D. is a good example of the conventional type. Don's a B student and a solid citizen in every respect. He's not flashy or a big talker. He's just a solid, dependable, hardworking guy. He watches the stock market and is more concerned about national politics than most students. His father is a manager in a big company, but Don has decided not to go into business. Instead, he wants to work for the federal government. He wants to work in accounting. Don plans to get married soon after graduation. He is especially concerned about having a good steady income for himself and his family.

The Enterprising Type

The enterprising type of person is energetic, enthusiastic, dominant, adventurous, and sometimes a little impulsive. Such people like to lead. They are interested in many kinds of activities—more than any other type. However, they usually are not too interested in manual work and do not like things that tie them down.

Enterprising people think well of themselves and like to have a good time. They consider themselves cheerful, persuasive, confident, aggressive, good speakers, and good leaders. They are interested in politics, status, and power. They admire leaders in industry and government. They may want to become politicians, salespeople, or promoters. They often want to start businesses of their own. They want to be their own bosses, and they're willing to take risks.

A good example is Julie N., who left college and took a job as an insurance sales representative. Within a few years, she was running her own agency. Bob T., another enterprising type, worked in a restaurant while he was in school. When he graduated, he borrowed some money and opened up a restaurant of his own. Both Julie and Bob were pretty good students, but they couldn't wait to get out of school. They were eager to get out into the world. To them, making a living was more of a game than an occupation. Enterprising types have big failures as well as big successes, but they're always optimistic about tomorrow.

The Artistic Type

People of this type are quite creative. They may be unusually skillful in writing, music, or art. Daydreams and creative expression are more important to them than sports, politics, or shop activities. Such people may not be too sociable, but they can be good talkers in their fields of interest.

The artistic type's self-image would include being sensitive, thoughtful, flexible, independent, unconventional, impulsive, achieving, and sometimes a little irresponsible. In spite of low self-ratings in popularity, they feel quite self-confident. Recognition for artistic achievements is more desired than power over others. Writers, opera stars, or famous painters are among their heroes. Many artistic people would like to become artists, writers, or designers of some kind.

Mary S. is a good example of the artistic type. She is an artist, although not all artistic people are. Mary's outstanding quality is the way she fills her life with beauty. She has a taste, a touch, a grace, that is not at all common. For her, every thing, every event, is to be savored and enjoyed for its own sake. She happens to be a rather quiet person, but you always know she's there. She fills the room with her presence. In her calm, quiet way, Mary gets a very great deal out of life.

Why Discuss Personality Types?

The purpose of discussing personality types is not to put you into a tight little group or type. Rather, it is to help you do some thinking about yourself. What are your outstanding personal qualities? Why not make a list? Ignore the six basic types for a moment. Browse through the qualities listed under the various types. Then jot down the qualities that you seem to have. Are you sensitive, flexible, independent, and radical? Or are you really something quite different?

Then think about your attitudes. How do you really feel about working with tools and machines? Would you rather work with words than with things? Do you truly enjoy working with people, or is this just something you sometimes say because it's what you're supposed to say? Do you really want the worries and responsibilities of being a leader? What kinds of activities do you really enjoy?

It also might be helpful to make another list of qualities you do not have, and of things you do not enjoy. Sometimes it's easier to say what we aren't than to say what we are. So make a list. Examine it carefully. Change it if it's not right. Focus on what you are and what you're not.

Whatever you discover about yourself is fine. No one is suggesting that one set of personal qualities is better than another. This exercise has nothing to do with good and bad. The whole point is that self-study can help you make a better match between yourself and your future career. And anything you can do to make a better match is well worth the effort.

A Brief Review

Where do all these ideas leave us? Let's take a few moments for review.

Personality Types   In this chapter, we have tried to make some sense out of the differences and similarities among people. We did this by grouping people according to like qualities of personality. We then tried to describe the general characteristics of people in each group. You may not fit precisely into any group. That doesn't matter. What does matter is that you discover more about yourself so you can choose an occupation that is suitable for you.

Suppose you have qualities that spill over into two or more of our personality groups. That may make it a little harder for you to choose an occupation. On the other hand, having a mixed set of qualities may be a fortunate thing. It suggests that you might be happy and successful in several kinds of work.

Human Needs   Our consideration of personality types emphasized the differences among groups of people. When discussing human needs in Chapter 3, we emphasized the similarities of people. As we have seen, many experts believe that people are driven by their needs, and that all people share the same needs. Although we may do different things, or do the same things in different ways, we all are striving toward the same goals. We all need to survive, to be safe, to belong, to be respected, and to make something of ourselves.

Yet because we have different backgrounds, abilities, and interests, our need pyramids do vary. Each of us must learn which needs drive us the most. Then we must try to find careers in which each of us can best satisfy our individual pattern of needs.

Parent, Child, and Adult   The states of being we discussed in Chapter 2 emphasize some of our problems. The need theory says, "Look, we all need those things." The Parent, Child, and Adult theory says, "I know, but certain forces are holding us back."

It's important for you to understand your Parent, your Child, and your Adult. Only then can you live like a grown-up person in today's world. You can't help having a Parent and a Child. They are there. But your Adult often can control these voices from the past if it understands them and really tries. Someone once said, "The more we understand the forces that shape us, the less we need to be their slaves."

The point is this: If your Adult is in control of you, and my Adult is in control of me, then we can look at each other and say, together, "We're OK." Let's be adults. Let's be alert and aware. Let's not be unwitting slaves to the past.

So who are you? Think about what we've said. Give it some serious thought. It could be the most important thinking you have ever done.

QUESTIONS FOR THOUGHT AND DISCUSSION

1. Susan Templeton has a realistic personality type. Her parents are urging her to become a computer programmer. Would Susan fit well into this occupation? Why or why not?

2. Tom Ramos has an artistic personality type. His parents want him to become the third family member to join the city fire department. What advice would you have for Tom?

3. There are many kinds of teachers—math teachers, English teachers, and gym teachers, to name only a few. Would all of these teachers ideally have the same type of personality? If so, what type would it be? If not, what would be the ideal personality type (or mix of types) for each kind of teacher?

4. To what extent do you think a person should think seriously about his or her personality type when considering possible careers?

5. Is it possible to be successful in a career without really being happy in it? If so, give an example of a person you know or have read about who is or was in that situation.

6. Which is the more important question: "How can I get more?" or "How can I live better?" Why?

What Is Work?

*Nothing is work unless you'd
rather be doing something else.*

Someone once said, "The world is full of willing people. Some are willing to work. The rest are willing to let them."

This makes *work* sound like a dirty word. Well, it's not. Everything the human race has ever achieved has been accomplished through work. Civilization depends upon it. Survival requires it. Yet there are problems connected with work.

One of the main problems arises when people get tied down to the wrong kind of work.

What is work, anyway? Well, *work* is one of those words that have many different meanings. Look in a big dictionary and you may find a whole page of definitions for *work*. Bread *works* when it rises. Wine *works* when it ferments. Engines *work*. Bees *work*. There are *works* of art. Students *work* math problems. This book is a *work*. Sometimes things don't *work* out the way you planned.

Obviously, *work* can mean many different things. It is one of those words that have different meanings for different people, and different meanings for the same person at different times.[1]

How can we make sense out of a word that means many different things? Tom is an aircraft mechanic, Jenny is a disc jockey, and Paul is a dental technician—yet they all claim to be working for a living. "Working for a living"—there's a clue! Whether a person is working or not depends less upon what that person is doing than upon his or her reasons for doing it.

Isn't it odd that nobody seems to "play" for a living? We work for a living, but we play for fun. Take basketball. When a young man in high school does it, we think of him as playing. Yet if this same young man later turns pro, basketball becomes his job. Suddenly he's working for a living. He's doing much the same thing, but while once it was play, now it is work. What changed? Mainly, the person's reasons for engaging in the sport changed.

A Definition and an Example or Two

With that thought in mind, let's suggest a meaning for work that may be new to you. *Work* can be defined as "something a person does for reasons outside the activity itself." By this definition, work is a means to an end; it is not an end in itself. We work in order to get something else that we need.

For example, if people work to build a bridge, they don't do it because they love to climb on high steel beams or pound rivets. They do it for pay and because they want the bridge for other purposes. The need theory would tell us that building the bridge will help them meet their needs. Which needs? Think about it. Can building a bridge help them survive? Can it help them be safe? Can it give them a feeling of belonging? Can they get esteem from building a bridge? Can building a bridge help them "actualize" themselves? If you don't see the connection between the bridge and the satisfaction of human needs, it might be a good idea to reread Chapter 3.

Take another example. In Southeast Asia, people work all day planting rice. Why? Because they love to bend their backs and walk in mud? Of course not. It's because they want the rice. And why do they want the rice? Because the rice helps them meet their need to stay alive.

So most people work, not because they love to do it, but because it produces something they need. If people do something just because they love doing it, and not because they're trying to get something by doing it, then they're not working.

According to this notion, many hobbies aren't work. Even a physical hobby like gardening isn't work if we do it just because we enjoy it. But the moment we do something not simply for the sake of doing it, but for some other reason, then we're working. So a gardener who plants and cultivates flowers to make a living is working. But a hobbyist who plants and cultivates an identical garden just because of a love for flowers isn't working. That person is doing something else.

The Work-Nonwork Sliding Scale

Actually, our definition of work stretches things a little. It deals with activities as though they were either/or. Either an activity is work for a person, or it isn't. In the real world, it usually isn't this clear-cut. It would be better for us to think of a sliding scale.

Such a scale would have pure work on one end and pure nonwork on the other, with a lot of possibilities in between. It might look something like Figure 4.

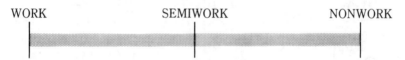

Figure 4 **The Work-Nonwork Sliding Scale**

We can place anything we do somewhere on this scale. Some things we do mainly to get an outside payoff. These would be near the work end of the scale. Waxing the car to impress our friends might be an example of this. We do other things for an inside payoff rather than for some outside payoff. These things would be near the nonwork end of the scale. Solving puzzles at home alone simply because we enjoy solving puzzles might be a mainly nonwork task. Many of the things we do would be nearer the middle of the scale. Preparing a Thanksgiving dinner for the family probably is near the semiwork part of the scale.

Of course, an activity that is near the work end of the scale for one person might be near the nonwork end for another. For example, building a stereo from a kit of parts might be very near the work end of the scale for Gus. He hates the task, but can't afford to buy a stereo already assembled. So he might do it because he really wants a new stereo.

For Judy, though, building the same stereo might be fun. It would almost be at the nonwork end of the scale for her. Why? Because in addition to wanting the set, she truly enjoys putting it together.

So building the set would be mostly work for Gus. But the very same task would be mainly nonwork for Judy. People differ.

What's the Point?

Why go into all this? There are three important points here. First, it was shown that work is a means to an end, and nonwork is an end in itself. Second, it was shown that many activities can be a mix of work and nonwork, depending upon a person's reasons for doing them. And third, it was shown that an activity that might be work for one person might be nonwork for someone else.

The main point is this: The chances are that you're going to spend most of your life making a living. There are many ways to make a living. For you, some of them would be close to the work end of the scale. You would do them, not because you enjoy them, but because you need the money. These are not good occupational choices for you. They would make you work too much.

Other ways of making a living would be around the middle of the scale for you. They would bring you money plus a limited amount of personal pleasure and satisfaction. These would not be bad career choices. They would be OK, satisfactory, average—the kind of career choices that most people actually make.

Finally, there can be some ways of making a living that would be very near the nonwork end of the scale for you. They would bring you a great deal of pleasure and satisfaction. Almost as a by-product, they also would bring you money.

If you are wise, you are going to choose this latter kind of occupation. Not only will it enable you to make a living, but it also will allow you to spend your time on the job doing things you truly enjoy.

If you enjoy tinkering with engines—if you're fascinated by how they operate and love their smooth precision, if you like the smell of grease, and if you have strong and sure hands—then why chain yourself to a desk?

On the other hand, if you like to plan things on paper, if you're good with words, if you enjoy analyzing numbers, if you like to work with others in solving human problems, then find an office occupation where you can do these things.

Both kinds of occupations are important. Society needs them both. One is not better than the other. The point is that people should discover what they really like to do. Then they should choose occupations that allow them to do those things. The person who does this will be taking a lot of the work out of life. That person also will gain many important satisfactions. Let's look at what a good occupational choice will do for you.

A Good Occupational Choice: What Will It Do for You?

A really good occupational choice will (1) provide you with adequate income, (2) give you security, (3) bring you real pleasure from your daily activities, (4) give you a feeling of importance, (5) give you some freedom on the job, and (6) provide you with an opportunity for personal growth.

If you make a good occupational choice, making a living won't be just work. You'll be one of those fortunate people who find deep satisfaction in doing the things that bring them their daily bread.

Let's face it: many people really do work for a living. Every day they do things they'd rather not do. Most of them are people who have made unfortunate occupational choices. This doesn't necessarily mean that their choices were totally bad. What it really means is that they could have made better choices.

But you need not make a poor occupational choice. You can make a good one if you know what you're doing and make an effort. To make a good occupational choice you must first understand yourself. Then you must understand the world of work. Finally, you must use your knowledge to make an intelligent match between yourself and a career.

Before we go on to talk about the world of work, let's emphasize one final point. We're not putting down anyone's occupation. All constructive occupations are helpful to society. Every occupation is right for some people. We need and respect people doing all occupations—especially when they do their jobs well.

What we are saying is that every person should seek an occupation that's right for himself or herself. It's right if the person is good at it and really enjoys doing it. A person who finds such an occupation can take much of the work out of making a living. As a result, that person can live a happier life.

So it really pays to find the right occupation for yourself. And in the process of looking for it, it pays to keep an open mind. Nobody can give you all the answers, even though some may try. You need to keep looking. You need to think for yourself. You need to be willing to change old ideas when better ones come along. As a wise man said, "It ain't the things you don't know that get you into trouble. It's the things you know for sure that ain't so." So keep looking. Keep your eyes—and your mind—wide open all the time.

OK, we're ready now to take a look at the American labor force as a whole. Then we will look at individual occupations.

QUESTIONS FOR THOUGHT AND DISCUSSION

1. How does work differ from nonwork? Give an example of each, from your personal point of view.

2. Give an example of an activity that would be work for you, but that would be nonwork or semiwork for one of your friends.

3. Give an example of an activity that would be nonwork for you, but that would be work for one of your friends. How do you account for the difference?

4. There is an old story about a tourist in Paris who saw two men constructing a building. The tourist asked the first man, "What are you doing?" The man replied, "I am laying bricks." The tourist then asked the second man, "What are you doing?" That man replied, "I am building a cathedral." What point do you see in this story?

5. Draw the Work-Nonwork Sliding Scale on a piece of paper and take it home. Ask your parents to check the point or range on the scale where they spend most of their time while on the job. Ask them if they would rather be spending their time somewhere else on the scale.

6. Is it possible for a person to have a job in which he or she doesn't have to work at all? If so, what job would that be? If not, what is the best that an average person can realistically hope for?

THE WORLD OF WORK

The World of Work

Our Labor Force

They advertised for workers,
but human beings came instead.

It's time to look at some facts and figures. A person really can't understand the world of work until he or she gets an idea of how big it is. You must know what is going on in the world of work, and the directions in which things are moving. Since it is easier to show these facts with numbers than with words, you will find some tables on the next few pages.

These tables will help you see the picture. To help yourself even more, draw some graphs using these numbers. The graphs may help you make good guesses about what will happen in the future.

There are thousands of charts, graphs, and tables telling about the United States labor force. Just a tiny part of this information—the part that should be most interesting and helpful to you—is shown here. All of the information comes from the *Monthly Labor Review,*[1] an official U.S. government publication.

The tables on the following pages will tell you four things:

1. How many people work, and how that number has changed since 1960.
2. Where people work, and how this has changed since 1960.
3. How much money workers in different industries make, and how wages have risen since 1960.
4. What kinds of workers tend to be unemployed.

How Many People Work?

Table 1 shows the size and growth of our civilian labor force since 1960.

Table 1 **HOW MANY PEOPLE WORK?**

Year	U.S. Population* 16 Yrs. & Over (Millions)	Civilian Labor Force** (Millions)	Civilian Labor Force Employed (Millions)	Unemployed
1960	119	72	68	4
1965	128	76	73	3
1970	139	85	81	4
1975	155	96	88	8
1980	169	109	101	8
1984	178	116	107	9

* *Does not include people in school.*
** *People 16 or over working or seeking work.*

What does Table 1 tell us? It tells us that the number of people 16 years of age and older grew by 59 million (50%) between 1960 and 1984. It tells us that the civilian labor force grew by 44 million (61%) during that same period. And among other things, it tells us that during those years the number of unemployed people grew by 5 million, a dramatic increase of 125%. The number of jobs simply has not kept pace with the increase in our population of working age. The unemployment problem has been especially severe since the mid-1970s, when an economic recession began.

A thoughtless person might say that Table 1 is just a bunch of numbers. A more mature person, however, would understand that the numbers stand for flesh-and-blood human beings—the working people of America. He or she would realize that almost every family in this country is touched in some way by recessions and their unemployment, and that recessions can reoccur.

This is not the place to discuss the many reasons for the recession of the 1970s and early 1980s. Our top economists still disagree on specific causes and their effects. Two things seem clear, however. First, better-trained people usually suffer less during a recession. And second, we should not blame technology for our problems. In the long run, improved technology always helps more than it hurts. Young people, especially, need to prepare themselves for the occupations of tomorrow. They should not restrict their thinking to the jobs of today.

It's interesting, though, that some people seem opposed to such progress. One example was the man who disliked the bulldozer because he thought it put people out of work. He and a friend were watching a highway being built. The man turned to his companion and said, "Look at that bulldozer over there. It's taking away the jobs of a hundred men with shovels." His friend replied, "Yes, or the jobs of a thousand men with spoons." A similar story could be told about the computer.

No one would deny that many problems arise from technological change. Technological advances aren't free. They come at a price. Sometimes they do put people temporarily out of work. But let's not condemn these advances too harshly. Remember that becoming more efficient in our work, being more productive, and lifting toil from human backs is one of the major ways of improving our society and our world. People can be retrained. A thinking person will always welcome a better tool.

However you look at it, Table 1 tells you what you can expect. You're going out into the world of work with millions of other people. All of them are scrambling for the best jobs they can find. Their work will keep changing as technology changes. And there may always be some who would like to work but can't find a job that fits.

Where Do People Work?

You now know how many people have jobs. You also know how these figures compare with the number of working-age people in the country. If you have done a little arithmetic, you've seen that 65% of the people over 16 who are not in school are in the civilian labor force. What happened to the others? Why isn't everyone in the labor force? Does the percentage of people in the labor force seem to be growing or shrinking? Why? Does the increasing number of working women have anything to do with this?

Well, now that you've thought about the size of our labor force, let's ask the next question. Where do all these people work? This can be shown in many ways, and some of them are rather complicated. What we will do is use a simple breakdown that's provided by the U.S. Department of Labor. If you want more details, see any issue of the *Monthly Labor Review* or any other publication telling about the labor force. There is usually a good deal of change occurring in the labor market. Over the years, Americans keep shifting their places of employment. Take a look at Table 2.

Table 2   **WHERE DO PEOPLE WORK?***

Industry	1960	1965	1970	1975	1980	1984
Agriculture	5.3	4.3	3.5	3.4	3.3	3.3
Mining	.7	.6	.6	.8	1.0	1.0
Construction	2.9	3.2	3.5	3.5	4.3	4.3
Manufacturing	16.8	18.1	19.3	18.3	20.3	19.6
Transportation and Public Utilities	4.0	4.0	4.5	4.5	5.1	5.2
Wholesale and Retail Trade	11.4	12.7	15.0	17.0	20.3	21.8
Finance, Insurance, and Real Estate	2.6	3.0	3.6	4.2	5.2	5.7
Services**	7.4	9.0	11.5	13.9	17.9	20.1
Government	8.4	10.1	12.6	14.7	16.2	16.0

* *All figures in millions. Self-employed persons, proprietors, unpaid family workers, and domestic servants are not included.*
** *Includes people working in education, medical professions, restaurants and hotels, and in personal service jobs such as barbers, beauticians, etc.*

Table 2 tells us a great deal about how the different industries are growing or shrinking. Look at agriculture. Only about 62% as many people work in agriculture today as worked there in 1960. Why? Agriculture has become mechanized and more efficient. Our farmers have done a splendid job. Their output per hour worked has risen three times faster than the output in the nonfarm industries.

Mining provides a nice example of an industry whose employment is strongly affected by world events. Mining had been a declining industry for many years when suddenly the world was hit by the oil shocks of the 1970s. In response to higher oil prices, public utility plants began using less oil and more coal to generate electricity. Employment in mining then went up.

Employment in construction and transportation is growing, but not very fast. The recession of the early 1980s caused the dip in manufacturing employment shown for 1984. This figure may bounce back a little in the future.

Take a look at the employment figures in wholesale/retail trade and in services. Draw some graphs using this information and watch those curves shoot up. These are the growth areas within the American economy. Table 2 provides dramatic evidence of how our country is changing—from a producer of goods to a producer of services.

This may be a good time to stop and think about your future. Companies come and go. (Think of all the computer companies that have folded.) You've seen in Table 2 that industries also rise and fall. (Service industries are up, agriculture is down, manufacturing is up and down.) Would it be best for you to enter an industry that is growing, one that is holding steady, or one that is declining? That is a broad question, but it is one worth thinking about. Remember, though, that not all of the companies in a declining industry necessarily decline. Trends have been known to change.

It is also good to keep in mind that some occupations (secretarial, trucking, accounting, sales, and many others) are found in many different industries. If you are going to be an accountant or a salesperson, for example, you could choose to work in any of several industries.

Now let's move on to another important question: How much do people earn? I think you will be very interested in Table 3.

How Much Do People Earn?

In this table we'll see how much the average workers in our major industries earn. We'll see also how earnings have increased in recent years.

Table 3 gives us a lot of information. Before we get into it, though, remember that these figures are for ordinary working people. Supervisors, managers, and professionals—whose salaries would be higher—are not included. Farm workers have not been included because many of them get room and board along with their pay. It is hard to compare them with other employees.

Remember, too, that the figures are averages for the country as a whole and that pay varies from place to place. In many cases, pay is higher in the North and West, and lower in the South. Salaries in big cities tend to be higher than in small towns. Some jobs pay more than others. And of course, salaries for experienced people usually are higher than for beginners. All of these factors are hidden in the averages. Still, the averages can tell us quite a bit.

Table 3   **HOW MUCH DO PEOPLE EARN?***

Industry	1960	1965	1970	1975	1980	1984
Overall Average	$2.09	$2.46	$3.23	$4.53	$6.66	$8.33
Mining	2.60	2.92	3.85	5.95	9.17	11.58
Construction	3.07	3.70	5.24	7.31	9.94	12.03
Manufacturing	2.26	2.61	3.35	4.83	7.27	9.17
Transportation and Public Utilities	NA**	3.03	3.95	5.88	8.87	11.15
Wholesale and Retail Trade	1.71	2.04	2.72	3.73	5.48	6.66
Finance, Insurance, and Real Estate	2.02	2.39	3.07	4.06	5.79	7.62
Services	NA**	2.05	2.81	4.02	5.85	7.62

* *Average hourly earnings for nonsupervisory workers on private, nonagricultural payrolls.*
** *Information not available.*

Table 3 tells us that average pay has more than tripled since 1960. In some industries it has quadrupled. This table also tells us that pay varies a good deal from industry to industry. This may be something to keep in mind as you consider the industry in which you want to work.

There is much additional information implied in Table 3. Where labor unions are strong, the pay is higher. Industries where work often is temporary and insecure (like construction) tend to pay higher average wages. Industries that employ many low-skilled people tend to pay lower average wages. An industry like finance, which has many fringe benefits (paid holidays, paid vacations, health insurance, retirement pensions, and so forth) tends to pay lower base wages.

It is important to note that Table 3 contains information only about wages. A worker's total earnings include not only wages, but fringe benefits as well. Total earnings (wages plus benefits) are called *compensation*. Benefits have been growing faster than wages in recent years. For many workers, benefits now amount to 30% or even 40% of total earnings. Thus a person whose wage is $8.00 per hour may well have a total compensation rate of $10.50 per hour or more.

Ask your parents and friends about wages in your area. Check reference materials in the library. Remember, pay in different industries really does vary. And the same occupation may be paid more in one industry than in another.

Who Are the Unemployed?

There is one more thing to think about—the matter of unemployment. What is the unemployment picture? Which people hold on to their jobs when employment grows tight? Which people are laid off? Who can't get work at all? This takes us to Table 4. This table goes back only to 1974 because of space limitations and our need to look closely at what has happened to unemployment in quite recent years.

Table 4 **WHO ARE THE UNEMPLOYED?***

Category (Age, Sex, Race)	1974	1976	1978	1980	1982	1984
Total—All civilian workers	5.6%	7.7%	6.0%	7.1%	9.7%	7.5%
Men, 20 years and over	3.8	5.9	4.2	5.9	8.8	6.6
Women, 20 years and over	5.5	7.4	6.0	6.3	8.3	6.8
Both sexes, 16–19 years	16.0	19.0	16.3	17.7	23.2	18.9
White	5.0	7.0	5.2	6.3	8.6	6.5
Nonwhite	9.9	13.1	11.9	13.2	18.9	14.0**
Occupation						
White-collar workers, total	3.3	4.6	3.5	3.7	4.9	3.8†
Professional & technical	2.3	3.2	2.6	2.5	3.3	2.6
Mgrs. & administrators	1.8	3.1	2.1	2.4	3.5	2.7
Salesworkers	4.2	5.4	4.1	4.4	5.6	4.3
Clerical workers	4.6	6.4	4.9	5.3	7.0	5.4
Blue-collar workers, total	6.7	9.4	6.9	10.0	14.2	11.0
Craft and kindred	4.4	6.3	4.6	6.6	10.2	7.9
Operatives	7.5	10.8	8.1	12.2	17.7	13.7
Transport equip. operators	NA‡	7.7	5.2	8.8	11.7	9.0
Laborers	10.1	13.7	10.7	14.6	18.5	14.3
Industry						
Construction	10.6	15.6	10.6	14.2	20.0	14.3
Manufacturing	5.7	7.9	5.5	8.5	12.3	7.5
Transportation & utilities	3.2	5.0	3.7	4.9	6.8	5.5
Wholesale & retail trade	6.4	8.6	6.9	7.4	10.0	8.0
Finance & service	4.6	6.5	5.1	5.3	6.9	5.9

* *Average annual rates of unemployment, in percent.*
** *1984 figure is combined rate for black and Hispanic-origin people.*
† *Occupation data in 1984 column was estimated by author.*
‡ *Information not available.*

As you look at Table 4 you can see that unemployment in the United States has varied in recent years. In general, however, the unemployment rate has been on an upward trend. Here is evidence of a recession's impact upon the labor force. There was a time, not long ago, when it was felt that as long as the unemployment rate remained under 5%, our country was in pretty good shape. Today, many experts believe that unemployment will not go below 6% within the foreseeable future. It was, of course, over 10% for a while in 1982–83. Although the situation has improved since then, it is one that should cause every young person to stop and think. No one wants to be unemployed. But where are the stable jobs? What does it take to get one and keep it? Table 4 gives you some valuable clues.

Table 4 clearly shows the groups that suffer most from unemployment. They are teenagers (short on skills and experience), nonwhites (victims of discrimination), and lower-skilled blue-collar workers (laborers and semiskilled machine operators). As you grow older, you will move away from the unemployment problems of teenagers. If you are a nonwhite, you may have a long-term problem, although discrimination in this country is diminishing. If you wish to reduce your chances of being unemployed, your task is obvious. You must obtain education and training in fields that tend to be less affected by unemployment. What are those fields? They are high-skill blue-collar occupations and white-collar jobs of all kinds.

In addition, you should think carefully about the industry in which you choose to work. Table 4 suggests very strongly that your chances of being unemployed are higher in construction and manufacturing than in transportation, trade, or services. Do yourself a favor. Take the time to digest and heed the story told in Table 4.

How Things Are Changing

Now that you know the figures, here are a few more facts about changes in the world of work. Each of the following points is likely to affect you, for better or for worse.

- The workweek is getting shorter. People once worked 12 hours a day, six days a week in this country. Sometimes they worked more. Now the eight-hour day is standard, but even this is shrinking. For example, the average hours worked per week has dropped from 38.6 in 1960 to 35.3 in 1984.

- A number of interesting innovations are being attempted. Some firms are trying a four-day workweek, ranging anywhere from 32 to 40 hours in length. Some of these experiments have worked well, while others have not. We can expect more companies to try it in the future.

- "Flextime" has been used for several years by a number of forward-looking employers. Using Flextime, people can, within limits, begin and end the workday whenever they wish. For example, a person might be allowed to begin work anytime between 8:00 A.M. and 10:00 A.M., and then go home anytime between 4:00 P.M. and 6:00 P.M.—as soon as a full day's work has been completed. This may turn out to be a big improvement over the usual situation in which employees work rigid, fixed hours. Many employees like the plan.

    A cynical story about fixed working hours has been making the rounds. A young man supposedly said, "My new job makes me absolutely independent. I can get there anytime I want before eight, and can leave anytime I wish after five." This may change for many people in the future.

- The working year is getting shorter. People are getting more days of vacation each year. They are getting more holidays, more sick leave—more free time all around.

- The working life is getting shorter. More and more, people are staying in school longer and retiring earlier. This leaves fewer years in the middle for full-time work.

- People's mobility is increasing. People are moving more, from house to house and from job to job.

- Employment discrimination against people because of race, sex, age, religion, national origin, and education gradually is being reduced. We all will agree that this is good. People should be employed for what they can do, not because of what they are.

- Wages for jobs traditionally held by women are gradually becoming more fair, compared to pay for jobs held mainly by men. The issue, called "comparable worth," is now in the courts. Women are arguing for pay equal to the pay men receive for comparable, though not identical, work. Women are winning this battle, but it won't be over for a long time.

- More and more work is being done by and for the government. In 1982, government purchases of goods and services accounted for over a quarter of the jobs in our economy. Most of the recent growth in government has been at the state and local levels.

- Employment is increasing in service-producing industries and decreasing in goods-producing industries. Much of this is due to technological improvements and the attractiveness of imported products such as cars, shoes, and electronic equipment.

- Blue-collar jobs are decreasing, while white-collar jobs are increasing. At the same time, blue-collar and white-collar jobs are getting to be more alike. Some experts are now beginning to talk about a blend of the two—the gray-collar job.

- We are seeing more households having two or even three wage earners.

- We are witnessing an increase in the number of people who seek only part-time work.

- As people get higher and higher incomes, they may begin to demand high-quality handmade goods instead of machine-made goods. As this happens, there will be more and more jobs for skilled crafts workers of many kinds. The day of the cabinetmaker, the tailor, and the custom shoemaker or metalworker may be coming back.

What the Numbers Do Not Tell

The numbers in this chapter have told us quite a story. We know, of course, that they have been averages. And averages can hide a lot of things. Still, averages are very useful in our daily lives. There is one thing, though, that these figures about wages, employment, and unemployment do not touch upon at all. We will end this chapter with some comments on that subject. The subject is the "discouraged worker."

The government defines our labor force as being all persons 16 years of age or older who are working or seeking work. A person who is working is obviously in the labor force. So is an unemployed person who is looking for work. Note that to be counted as "unemployed," a nonworking person actually must be looking for a job. If a person is not working and not looking, he or she is not counted as being in the labor force.

Millions of people (nobody really knows how many) are not working, but would like to work. Nevertheless, they are not looking for jobs. Many of them looked and looked, but were unable to find work. Often, they looked for months and years. After a time, they became convinced that they could never find jobs. So they gave up and quit looking. They are no longer in the labor force. These people are the "discouraged workers" who are lost from our statistics.

These people may be young or old, male or female, with skin of any color. They are people who simply became so discouraged that they dropped out. Their experiences often are very sad. You may know such a person or—heaven forbid—someday you may be tempted to become one. Here is a story for such people. It is not a pleasant story, but it illustrates a point. It is a story about a psychologist who was experimenting with the behavior of fish.

The psychologist had a big aquarium. The tank was about 15 feet long, three feet high, and three feet wide. In the center of both side walls there was a slot that ran from top to bottom. These slots were directly across from each other. So if the experimenter wanted to, he could slide a glass separator into these slots and divide the tank into two parts.

One day he was experimenting with a fish called a northern pike. The pike was in the aquarium all alone, and the tank separator was out. So the pike was free to swim wherever it wanted. It did, and got well acquainted with the whole tank. There was only one problem—there was no food in the tank.

Several days went by. Still no food. More time passed. When the experimenter knew that the pike was really hungry, he did two things. First he put the separator in the tank. It was clear glass, and the pike could see through it. But while the fish once had been free to swim wherever it wanted, the pike now had to stay on one side because of the separator.

The second thing the experimenter did was to dump a bucket of minnows into the tank. Minnows are the pike's favorite food. The trouble was that while the pike was on one side of the separator, the minnows were put in on the other. The pike was starving, and it could see this food over on the other side of the tank. What do you think it did?

Well, it did just what you'd expect—it charged. The pike charged for the minnows, but unfortunately it didn't know much about glass separators. The pike charged head-on into that glass separator and smashed its nose. A little blood came.

But the pike wheeled around and charged again. No luck. It charged again. And again. And again. Still no luck. The pike was getting tired, but it kept trying. The fish actually charged that separator more than 50 times. Then—broken and bleeding —the pike gave up. It had determined that the food couldn't be gathered.

Then the experimenter took out the separator. Now the pike was in the tank with all those minnows. There was nothing to keep it from getting them. The minnows were brushing against its scales and swimming right before its eyes. But what did the pike do? Nothing!

The experience with the separator had taught the pike that the minnows could never be gotten. And, not wishing to be hurt anymore, the pike gave up. It just stayed in that tank and starved to death. Surrounded by food, the pike starved to death.

What's the point? People are not fish. They are smarter. Yet, if a person tries and tries but keeps getting hurt, what will happen? This is the way it has been for many people in the world of work. They've tried and tried, gotten hurt and hurt again, until some of them have given up. Let's hope you will never be one of these people.

Behind this story is a plea to the discouraged worker. Be brighter and more courageous than a fish. When things go wrong, don't just give up. Everything changes as time goes by. A discouraged person almost always has alternatives. He or she can change through training and become more employable. Help and advice can be sought. A person can become more persistent. Sights temporarily can be lowered a little. A great deal can be done by a person with imagination and courage. The key word here may be *courage*. A wise person once said, with only a little exaggeration, "Without courage, you are nothing."

QUESTIONS FOR THOUGHT AND DISCUSSION

1. Which grew more rapidly between 1960 and 1984—the population of the United States or our civilian labor force? What problem, if any, did this create?

2. Do you agree or disagree with the claim that we should not blame technological improvements for our unemployment problems? Why or why not?

3. In which industry did employment grow most rapidly between the years 1960 and 1984? In which industry did

employment grow most slowly? Did employment actually decline in any industry? If so, which? Why?

4. What is the difference, if any, between "wages" and "compensation"?

5. Which category of workers had the highest rate of unemployment in 1984? Did this same group also have the highest unemployment in other years? Why? What other groups also tend to have high rates of unemployment? Why? Which groups tend to have low unemployment? How do you account for that?

6. In which industry were average wages highest in 1984? In which industry were they the lowest? How do you account for the wage differences between industries?

7. What is "Flextime"? Would you like to work under such a system? Why or why not?

8. Suppose we divided all industries into two groups—those that produce goods and those that produce services. Which group is growing? Which is declining? How do you account for that? How might this affect your occupational choice?

DANCER
NURSE
Engineer
Secretary
BANKER
TEACHER
DIETITIAN
DESIGNER
Beautician
C.P.A.
JEWELER
D.D.S.
Actress
LAWYER
COMPUTER PROGRAMMER
ECOLOGIST
FARMER
COUNSELOR

The World of Work

20,000 Occupations

*Knowledge without wisdom is a
load of books on the back of an ass.*

We have been discussing facts about our labor force in a general way. People who are trying to make occupational choices need a general idea of where people work, how much they earn, and so forth. But they also need specific information. Especially important is information about the many kinds of occupations that exist.

There are far more occupations than many people think. There are thousands of occupations that most of us know nothing about. Look at it this way. There are about 240 million people living in the United States. As you know, about 116 million of them are in the labor force. What you probably don't know is that these 116 million people are working at more than 20,000 different occupations.

Think about that. More than 20,000 occupations! One of these days you will have to choose an occupation. Which one will it be? How many of the 20,000 possibilities have you thought about? How many of them have you even heard about?

This chapter will tell you where you can find out about those 20,000 occupations. First we will discuss some useful books. Then we will identify people who can give you help.

The Dictionary of Occupational Titles

The *Dictionary of Occupational Titles*[1] (*DOT* for short) is the most basic source of information about occupations in the

United States. Many people turn to it when they want to know about jobs. Your school library probably has a copy of the *DOT*. Take a look at it the first time you get a chance.

The *DOT* is a lot more than an ordinary dictionary that defines words. It lists every occupation in the country. It also explains what is done in each occupation, how it is done, and why it is done. The *DOT* describes the aptitudes a person needs for each occupation. It explains the interests and personalities that fit well with each occupation. It tells about the physical demands of each occupation. It describes the conditions under which each occupation is performed.

The information given about each occupation is brief, but a lot is said in a small amount of space. As you look through the *DOT,* you'll see that each occupation has been given a code number. This code is used to classify occupations into groups. The *DOT* uses nine basic occupational groups. These are identified as follows:

0/1   Professional, technical, and managerial
 occupations

 2   Clerical and sales occupations

 3   Service occupations

 4   Agriculture, fishery, forestry, and related
 occupations

 5   Processing occupations

 6   Machine trades occupations

 7   Benchwork occupations

 8   Structural work occupations

 9   Miscellaneous occupations

Here is a good way to begin thinking about occupations. First, consider which one of the nine occupational groups interests you most. Then find out about specific occupations in that group.

Ask your teacher to discuss the *DOT* in class. It has some amazing things in it. For example, did you know that there are at least 18 different kinds of carpenters? Also, there are at least seven kinds of lawyers, and over 200 different kinds of salespeople.

Just for fun, thumb through the A's and the P's in the *DOT* alphabetical index. This will give you a sample of occupations. Here are some of the listings you will find:

Under A	Under P
Accordion maker	Package designer
Acid dumper	Parachute folder
Acrobatic dancer	Park ranger
Air-traffic coordinator	Pearl stringer
Alley cleaner	Pharmacist
Animal ecologist	Pickle pumper
Antisqueak filler	Pipe-cleaning machine operator
Arbitrator	Plaster molder
Artificial-glass-eye maker	Pocket presser
Art librarian	Powder mixer
Asparagus sorter	Prospecting driller
Azalea grower	Puppeteer

There's much more, of course. It's all there. As you look through the *DOT,* you have the whole world of occupations in your hands.

Occupational Clusters

As you might expect, 20,000 occupations can be grouped in many ways. The *DOT* uses the U.S. Department of Labor's nine coded groupings. Other people group the occupations in other ways. For example, the U.S. Office of Education has divided them into 15 occupational clusters. Perhaps you've heard something about these clusters in your school. The list is given on page 70.

U.S. Office of Education Occupational Clusters

Agribusiness and
Natural Resources
Business and Office
Health
Public Service
Environment

Communication
and Media
Hospitality and
Recreation
Manufacturing
Marine Science
Marketing and
Distribution

Personal Service
Construction
Transportation
Consumer and
Homemaking
Fine Arts and
Humanities

Many schools are designing educational programs around these clusters. Such schools are trying to help students prepare for careers in a sensible way. The idea is that a student first should find a cluster of occupations that is appealing. Then the student should decide which specific occupation within that cluster he or she really wants to enter. This saves the student from getting lost in an unorganized mass of 20,000 different occupations.

These clusters of occupations should help as you think about your future job. You also might think about the way occupations are grouped in the *DOT*. There seems to be one main difference between the *DOT*'s nine groups and the Office of Education's 15 clusters. The nine groups tend to focus on what people do, while the 15 clusters emphasize industries where people work.

The Occupational Outlook Handbook

As you have seen, the *DOT* can give you a bird's-eye view of all the jobs in the country. This view is very helpful as you begin to study the world of work. However, when you want the full story on a particular job, a bird's-eye view is not enough. This is where another U.S. Department of Labor publication comes in. This one is called the *Occupational Outlook Handbook.*[2]

This book (let's call it *OOH* for short) is keyed to the *DOT* and uses the same code numbers. But instead of giving a brief write-up on every job as the *DOT* does, the *OOH* gives much more thorough descriptions of a smaller number of jobs. The *OOH* describes about 200 of the most popular occupations in the country. Each of these occupations gets a two-page write-up in the *OOH*. If an occupation interests you, it may be written up in the *OOH*.

A new edition of the *OOH* is published every two years. Since the job market constantly changes, the Department of Labor also publishes a magazine called the *Occupational Outlook Quarterly*.[3] This magazine updates the information in the *OOH*. It is published four times a year.

What occupations does the *OOH* cover? Here's a small sample from its group of occupational clusters:

Administrative and Managerial Occupations
Accountants
Hotel managers
Purchasing agents
School administrators

Natural Scientists and Mathematicians
Computer systems analysts
Statisticians
Chemists
Foresters

Social Scientists, Social Workers, Religious Workers, and Lawyers
Economists
Psychologists
Recreation workers
Ministers

Service Occupations
Firefighters
Cooks and chefs
Medical assistants
Flight attendants

Administrative Support Occupations, Including Clerical
Bank tellers
Mail carriers and postal clerks
Secretaries and stenographers
Computer operating personnel

Construction and Extractive Occupations
Carpenters
Ironworkers
Plumbers and pipefitters
Coal miners

Production Occupations
Assembler occupations
Furniture upholsterers
Machine tool operators
Welders and flamecutters

Transportation and Material Moving Occupations
Bus drivers
Truck drivers
Airplane pilots
Ambulance drivers and attendants

What does the *OOH* say about each occupation? For some good clues, consider the headings used in its write-ups:

Nature of the Work
Working Conditions
Employment
Training, Other Qualifications,
    and Advancement
Job Outlook
Earnings
Related Occupations
Sources of Additional Information

This is exactly the information a person would want to have while searching for an occupation. The *OOH* doesn't try to sell you on any particular occupation. It doesn't build any job up or put any job down. It just gives you the facts. It tells you what to expect in that occupation during the next eight or ten years. It is true that nobody knows the future. But the *OOH* gives you the opinions of some of the top labor experts in the country.

So spend some time with the *OOH*. Every good school library should have a copy. Ask your teacher to talk about it in class. This could be one of your best sources of information.

Other Sources of Published Information

Where else can you go for help? Look in your library's card catalog. Look under the headings *Occupational Information, Vocational Guidance,* and *Vocational Education.* Many books have been written about occupations, but most of them are a little difficult to read. Some of the easier popular books were written by Richard Bolles,[4] Anna Burke,[5] Gail Sheehy,[6] and Studs Terkel.[7]

Your library also may have a number of pamphlets on occupations. Business firms, labor unions, professional organizations, and government agencies publish these pamphlets. The Bureau of Labor Statistics puts out occasional occupational bulletins. The U.S. Department of Education publishes a lot of information. Your library may have films and tapes on occupations. Ask your librarian to help you find material.

People Who Can Help

You can learn much about occupations by talking with people. In school, there are three people to see—your teacher, your librarian, and your counselor. Each of them can help in a special way. Of the three, your counselor probably has had the most training in occupations and career choice. If you haven't met the counselor yet, go in and get acquainted. The counselor is there to help you. Don't be afraid to take some tests if they are suggested. These tests can tell you much about yourself, your interests, and your abilities.

Talk with your parents. Talk with your parents' friends. Talk with relatives. Talk with people who actually are working in jobs that interest you. Take field trips if your teacher can arrange them. Most people are glad to help a student who has a good attitude and really wants to learn.

Finally, if you get a chance to work part-time at or around a job that interests you, don't walk—run—and take it. Doing a job or at least seeing it done can be more enlightening than just reading or hearing about it.

Remember that finding out about careers requires you to do something. You cannot sit and wait for the information to come to you. Just sitting around will hurt you by limiting your knowledge. Suppose nothing good comes your way?

A farmer doesn't just harvest whatever happens to grow in the field. To get a good crop you must plant seeds and work in the field. If you want to harvest a good occupation, you'll have to make an effort. Other people can tell you about soil and rain, seed, tools, and fertilizer. But you'll have to work the field yourself.

QUESTIONS FOR THOUGHT AND DISCUSSION

1. What is the most basic source of information about the 20,000 jobs in the United States? What kinds of information about jobs does this publication contain?

2. Where could you find more complete information about one of the 200 most popular jobs? Exactly what kinds of information does this book contain?

3. Suppose you needed still more information than is contained in the above two sources. Under which card catalog headings would you look in your library?

4. Where in *this* book can you find the names of many sources of additional information about occupations and occupational choice?

5. Name five places, in addition to books, where you can get information about occupations and occupational choice. How many of these sources are available to you? How many have you used?

6. Is there one best source of occupational information? If so, what is that source? If not, why not?

Choosing Your Occupation

Key Ideas

*A life without a plan
is likely to become driftwood.*

Choosing your occupation should not mean taking the first job that comes along. Choosing an occupation should mean finding the best possible match of yourself with a particular kind of work. If you want to make a good match, you have to make an effort.

Many people do not put enough effort into choosing their careers. No one really knows how many people in this country are in the wrong jobs. The number, however, is high. In a recent survey, 47% of the people interviewed said their jobs were uninteresting. Thirty-one percent said they would quit if they could afford to.

Our labor turnover figures show this dissatisfaction. Employee turnover in the United States averages about 3% per month. People change jobs for many reasons, but 3% per month is a lot of job changing. Why does it happen? You could blame the jobs. You could blame the workers. But it may be best to blame the match between workers and their jobs.

Why do we have so many poor matches? One big reason is that many people choose jobs without having enough information about (1) themselves, (2) occupations, or (3) both.

It is tragic that this is how so many people make career decisions. Some people don't know where to look. Some never stop to think about the importance of their career choices. Some may be lazy. And all of them are dealing with a very hard problem. It's not easy to make a good career choice.

The Odds

Actually, the odds do not favor making a really good career choice. Look at Figure 5.

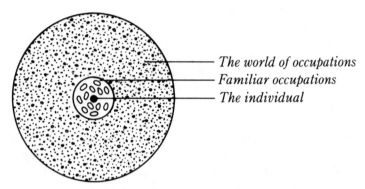

Figure 5   **The World of Occupations**

The dot in the center is the individual. The area within the big circle is the world of occupations. All 20,000 occupations listed in the *DOT* are contained within that circle. How many of those occupations does the average person actually see? An exact number can't be given, of course. But what an individual often sees is only a few occupations. These are the jobs that are personally familiar to the individual. They are the jobs held by parents, friends, relatives, and neighbors. They also may include a few others that the individual may have read about or seen on TV. Altogether, the person may be aware of a few dozen occupations. These are contained within the smaller circle in Figure 5.

That's a tragic situation. Of the 20,000 occupations available, the average person knows about a few dozen. Usually, he or she makes a job choice from just a few of the many possibilities. No one can choose an occupation if he or she doesn't know that it exists.

What this means is that the ordinary person really lives in a tight little circle of familiar jobs rather than in the total world of occupations. Such a person is a prisoner, walled in by a lack of information.

We're all prisoners. Yet we can enlarge our prisons by enlarging our knowledge. Suppose a person who knows about 30 occupations takes the time to learn about 30 more. Then his or her career possibilities will be twice as great. That person becomes freer and multiplies his or her chances of making a good career choice.

By now you can see why we spent so much time discussing the *DOT,* the *OOH,* and other sources of job information. Those sources expose you to many occupations that you may never have heard about. A newly discovered job just might be much better for you than any you have thought about before.

Note that we have been talking about making good or very good career choices. A very good choice is about the best most people can hope for. For most of us, perfection is out of reach. What is a very good occupational choice? Well, it was described in Chapter 5, on page 48. But let's go over it once again. A very good occupational choice is one that will (1) provide you with adequate income, (2) give you security, (3) bring you real pleasure from your daily activities, (4) give you a feeling of importance, (5) give you some freedom on the job, and (6) provide you with an opportunity for personal growth. The more of these things a job provides for you, the better the job will be for you. If you stop to think about these goals, you will see that they go right back to human needs.

An idealist might decide to seek the best of all possible jobs for himself or herself. While that may be a worthy goal, it's also a little unrealistic. A person could spend a lifetime looking for that one best job without ever finding it. How would it be recognized, even if it were found? So don't be unrealistic. Think about making a career choice that is "only" very good for you.

In a rough way we can compare career choices with grades in school. The typical grade—and the typical career choice—is a C. A grade of C is all right. It is average and will get a person by. But it's usually nothing to brag about. Most people make C-type job choices and then go on to live C-type lives. Such lives, while not bad, are not great, either.

Some people make career choices that are D's and F's. These are the job drifters, the failures. They are the people who show up every few months in the turnover statistics. If we were talking about marriages, these would be the people who keep turning up in the divorce courts. They make poor choices and have to pay the consequences.

And then there are the people who make good or very good career choices. We can consider these choices to be A's or B's. The people who make these choices are those who tend to get the most out of life. Their choices are made after careful study and thought or through a stroke of sheer luck. But it's risky to rely on luck in choosing a career. The stakes are too high. By making an effort, you can be more sure of the result. So take your time, and choose your occupation. Don't let some occupation choose you.

It's not hard to see why so many people get C's. They put very little effort into making their job decisions. They just drift into careers. Yet many of them do succeed to some extent. What saves most of these people is the fact that human beings can be multipurpose machines. Most of us are adaptable. Many of us can learn to do C-type work in a fairly wide variety of jobs. But is a C really good enough for you?

Almost every adult has done reasonably well on a number of different jobs. For example, there is a man who started out delivering papers. Then he went on to be a grocery clerk, a termite exterminator, an electrician, a naval officer, a business manager, and a college professor. He was fairly successful in all of these jobs, even though they were not much alike. This man is not very special. Most people can get C's in a number of jobs. But you should not settle for that. Your goal should be to find a career where you can get an A.

Often people enter occupations because the pay is good. Later, these people drop out because they don't like the work. But why build up a record of disappointments? Wouldn't it be better to know more about the work before taking a job in the first place?

The experts keep piling up evidence. It shows that no matter how much they are paid, people are not likely to be happy with their jobs if they don't enjoy the work itself. If a job choice is to be more than a C, there has to be a better-than-average match between the person and the work.

Knowing Yourself

This brings us back to the individual person. Philosophers through the ages have been telling people, "Know thyself." If this were an easy task, we wouldn't need so many reminders to do it. It's not easy to know ourselves. Most of us go through our lives without fully discovering who and what we are. One of the reasons, of course, is that we keep growing and changing. But we need to make the effort, and the only place to begin is where we are right now.

A helpful thing for you to do right now would be to study your interests, skills, and aptitudes. Take the vocational aptitude and interest tests that are given in your school. These tests will not answer all your questions. They can, however, offer you some clues. Talk over the results with your counselor. Find jobs in the *DOT* and the *OOH* that interest you. Then compare your interests, skills, and aptitudes with those required for the jobs you've chosen. Make a list of things you're really good at.

Make a list of questions that will tell you something about yourself. Then, answer the questions truthfully. For example, you might ask yourself:

Do I prefer working indoors or outdoors?

Do I prefer physical work to mental work, or vice versa?

Do I prefer working alone or as a member of a group?

Do I like to move around or work in one place?

Do I prefer working with papers or with products?

Do I like to lead others, or do I prefer to be led?

Do I like to persuade people to do things?

Do I like to take risks?

Do I have a strong need to be secure?

Do I like to create things with my hands?

Do I like to work with machines?

Do I like to work with numbers?

Do I enjoy a lot of variety in my work?

Do I like work that really makes me think?

Do I like to work at helping people?

There's nothing magic about this set of questions. If you check your library you will find other lists. Some of those lists may be more useful to you than this one. The idea is not to sell you on any one set of questions. The idea is to get you to think seriously about yourself and the things you really would like to do for the next 40 years.

That's right—40 years. That's the average length of a career. Sometimes it's even longer. No one should start out on a 40-year journey that won't be enjoyable. So be honest. Don't kid yourself about yourself. It doesn't pay. A person rarely succeeds at anything unless he or she enjoys doing it.

Location

There's yet another matter a person should consider when choosing an occupation. That's the matter of location—the actual physical location of the work. Many people restrict their lives by refusing to go where their best job choices are located. Many occupations are not spread evenly across the country. Some occupations are found in pockets, here and there, and hardly exist anywhere else.

For example, automotive designers are concentrated in Detroit. Rubber workers are concentrated in Ohio. Many jobs for electronics engineers are found near Boston and in California. Many aircraft engineers find work around Los Angeles.

Oil workers find jobs mainly in Texas, Alaska, and Oklahoma. This does not necessarily mean that these occupations are found only in those places. But it does mean that your chance of getting one of those jobs is much better where the jobs are concentrated. So people sometimes have to relocate to the areas where particular jobs are plentiful.

Moving has its costs, in dollars and in human relationships. Few who have moved would deny that. Yet people move every day. They hope to get better jobs, live in more attractive communities, and enrich their lives. Young people who are not yet tied down should pay special attention to this. They would be wise to weigh the pros and cons of moving to where the best job opportunities are. They may not be doing themselves a favor by limiting themselves to local job opportunities. A person who remains at home should have strong reasons for doing so. People who want to broaden their range of choices may have to consider a broader range of job locations.

It could be that the best job opportunity for a certain person is right there at home. But often that is not the case. Through a lack of action or a lack of careful thought, many young people restrict their career opportunities to those found in one or a few places. When they do that, they are drawing the prison walls closer in on themselves.

You may have heard someone say something like, "I wouldn't move to Chicago (or some other place) for anything in the world. I want to live and die right here." But when you ask if they have ever lived in Chicago (or wherever) the answer often is, "Why, no. I've never been there, but I've heard about it." When you check further you often find that they heard about the place from a friend. The friend once spent two days there on a fast vacation. Yet on the basis of such information, many people rule out hundreds of good job opportunities.

The point is that when you rule out a place, you cut yourself off. That's all right if you really know what you're doing. But many people seem to do it without much thought. They blindly cut themselves off from what might truly be golden opportunities.

Like people, places differ. Talk to someone who's lived in many places. You'll find that there's no such thing as a perfect place. Every place has its good points and its bad points. What you do when you move is expose yourself to a new mixture of good and bad. But you still have some of both.

Location alone seldom makes a person happy or satisfied. It's a factor, but it's only one of many. The job itself tends to be more important than the place in which it's found. And of course, the people in a place are important, too.

Still, you often can better yourself by moving to a new location. You owe it to yourself to find out where the opportunities are. Before moving, consider carefully the nature of the job to which you are going. Think about the effects the move will have on others as well as upon yourself.

Timing

The time to make your occupational choice is when you are ready to make it. You are ready when more knowledge about yourself and occupations will not be likely to lead to a better decision. Some people are ready to make their decisions when they are in high school. Others become ready when they are in college. And a few never seem ready or able to make an intelligent job choice.

Age, by itself, may not have much to do with a person's readiness to make a wise career choice. Knowledge and the ability to make sound judgments are the key factors. Young people should not be pushed to make career choices too soon. On the other hand, young people should begin early to explore careers. They should not postpone their decisions unnecessarily.

The pressures on young people usually are for too-early decisions. For example, a ninth-grade student was urged by her teacher to enter a certain career. The student's parents tried to push her into another field. Neither the teacher nor the parents urged the young woman to explore other possibilities. They simply felt that they knew what was best for her. Such people mean well. A young person would be wise to listen carefully to their advice. The reasoning behind the advice is especially valuable. But such advice is just one part of the total information one needs before choosing a career. Input from many sources, not from just one or two, is needed to make a good career choice.

Most mistakes made in occupational decisions probably come from making decisions too early. Often young people make decisions before they've made a good search. Then they lock themselves into educational programs to prepare for the wrong occupations. Later they may either recognize (and pay for) costly mistakes, or else go into careers for which they are not well suited. It is better to delay a decision than to end up in a situation like that.

Occupations chosen early tend to be the ones that are seen every day. Less visible occupations are chosen later or not at all. For example, a study was made of when people in three different careers decided to enter their occupations. The subjects were groups of people who had gone into teaching, business, and chemistry. Which group do you think made its occupational choices earliest?

The teachers did. Teaching is a highly visible occupation. The people who went into teaching had decided while in high school to become teachers.

The people who became chemists didn't make their career choices until they were well along in college. There were several reasons for this, but one reason was more important than others. This was the fact that chemistry did not really become visible to these people as a profession until they studied the subject in college. If they had rushed to make career choices while in high school, perhaps none of them would have become chemists.

The people working in business held a variety of jobs. Most of them had not finished college. They were managers, administrative assistants, and secretaries. There was no clear pattern in the timing of their career choices. Apparently many had drifted into their jobs. They didn't seem to expect to make careers of their occupations.

Your occupational choice should be made when you are ready to make it. This could be while you are in high school. It could be while you are in college. It could even be after you have finished college. The timing depends on you.

All things considered, it's probably better to be a little late than too early. If you choose too early, you are likely not to consider all the factors involved. A period of travel before you decide on a firm choice can be helpful. Take time to look around. The bigger your net, the better your chance of landing something good.

Occupations and Education

Career education in our schools is getting better. The many programs that help young people explore occupations are on the right track. They encourage students to read. They discuss careers. They encourage young people to get out into the world and see what's going on. They urge students to see for themselves what people working in various careers actually do.

Recently, many schools have placed a new emphasis on vocational education. This has created new opportunities for many students who do not plan to go to college. The emphasis on vocational training varies from school to school. But making vocational courses available will almost certainly help a lot of students as they search for suitable careers.

The formal education required for many jobs ends with high school graduation. Other occupations require training in a two-year college or technical school. Still other jobs require four or more years of college. Perhaps you have already made a tentative career choice. You may also have decided how far you will go in school. Even so, it would be smart to stay alert for additional career information. One always should be willing to reconsider plans in light of new data. Occupational plans and educational plans tend to change together.

Advanced Training

Many people choose jobs that require training beyond high school. Then it is necessary to choose a place to get this training. Choosing the right school and/or training program involves another search. There are usually fewer alternatives to consider when selecting schools than when selecting occupations.

Your counselor and the school library have information about schools and training programs. Study this material carefully. There are great differences in schools and training programs. So be sure to talk with the people who know about these things before you make a decision. If you can actually visit the schools you are considering, so much the better.

Changes

There are a number of changes going on in the areas of occupations and education. One of these has to do with the amount of education needed for various occupations.

We have gone through a period in which there was a heavy emphasis on the college degree. People were getting degrees, and employers demanded degrees of people who applied for jobs. Often the degrees weren't really necessary to do the work. The educational requirements for jobs were just too high. As a result, many college-trained people were hired for jobs they soon found to be boring. At the same time, many people with less education were unable to get jobs that they could have performed perfectly well.

This is now changing. More and more, people are being hired simply on the strength of their ability to do the work. The amount of time spent in school is becoming less important. "Can you do the job?" is the question today.

Also, we are developing a new respect for people who work with their hands. We are coming to see that not a wheel can turn without the brains and muscle of blue-collar workers. You may be interested in and suited for a skilled trade. You may want to work as a carpenter, an electrician, a plumber, a mason, and so forth. If this is where your skills and interests lie, don't hesitate to become an apprentice in one of these fields. You will find satisfying work, good pay, and increasing respect for your skills.

You may be thinking of going to a two-year college for training. You are in good company. Thousands of bright young people are going to two-year colleges. Their educations will prepare them for satisfying, well-paying careers. Many two-year colleges are new, but their graduates are well trained. And employers want those graduates badly.

Now a word about the future. The world is changing rapidly. A person probably should expect to work at more than one job during a lifetime. The occupation you choose now is very important. Still, it may not be the one you have when you retire. Having several different occupations could make your life more interesting. It is not impossible to correct mistakes or to try new things. But you should realize that a new job may require new training. You may be going back to school to prepare for a new job. In fact, you may find yourself back in school several times during your career. Education and training are likely to be permanent parts of your life.

Now let us look at an actual method for making your first occupational choice. If that choice is a good one, you may not have to make a lot of changes that could slow down the progress of your career.

QUESTIONS FOR THOUGHT AND DISCUSSION

1. What does this chapter say is the major reason for the high employee turnover in the United States? Do you agree? Why or why not?

2. If people were graded on their career choices, most people would get C's. How do people who get A's and B's on their job choices differ from those who get C's?

3. What recommendation does this chapter make about being willing to move in order to find good jobs? What dangers or risks, if any, are there in moving?

4. When should a person make his or her occupational choice? Does this depend mainly on a person's age, or mainly on something else? If something else, what is it?

5. What kinds of jobs tend to be chosen earliest in life? What kinds of jobs tend to be chosen later? Why?

6. Tell whether this statement is true or false: "If a person wants to get a good job, he or she simply must obtain a college degree." Explain your answer.

POINT SYSTEM
OCCUPATION EVALUATION SHEET

Degree Codes

Provided by the job:
5 = To a great extent
4 = To a large extent
3 = To an average extent
2 = To a low-average extent
1 = To a small extent

Occupation: _____

Factors	Degree	Multiplier	Weighted Points
Adequate Income			
Security			
Pleasure from Daily Activities			
Feeling of Importance			
Freedom on the Job			
Opportunity for Personal Growth			
Other			
Other			
Other			
Other			
		Total Weighted Points: _____	

Choosing Your Occupation

How to Do It

The first step toward greatness is to be honest.

Everything we've discussed up to now has been designed to bring you to this point. In this chapter we explore practical, "how-to" methods for choosing your occupation.

A "how-to" experience is exciting. Yet before you try to do anything, you should be prepared. That is why we've spent a lot of time getting you ready for this experience. If you have mastered the previous chapters, you are ready. This chapter is about decision making.

Decision Making

In a way, this entire book is about decision making. It is designed to help you decide upon your occupation, one of your most important decisions. But in this chapter we're getting specific. We will consider in detail what happens when a person makes a decision.

The decision-making process goes like this:

1. *Define your objective.* In this case, let's say that your objective is to live the best possible life.
2. *Identify your problem.* The problem here is choosing your occupation. If you arrive at a good solution to this problem, you will have taken a big step toward reaching your objective.

3. *Gather information.* You need certain information to solve this problem. You must learn about yourself and about occupations. The more good information you get, the better.
4. *Evaluate the information.* Study the information carefully. Eliminate any that's not useful. Keep everything that will help you solve the problem.
5. *Narrow down the possible solutions.* You need to focus on the few most promising solutions. This means ruling out a lot of unrealistic occupations. Leave yourself with only the good possibilities.
6. *Study the remaining possibilities very carefully.* Get all the information you can about them—in-depth information.
7. *Make the best decision.* Choose the occupation that, all things considered, seems best for you.
8. *Follow up.* After you've made a decision, keep your eyes and ears open. Carefully observe how things are working out. In spite of all your effort, you could have made a mistake.
9. *Decide again.* If your follow-up tells you that you have made the correct decision, keep going. You are on your way. But if the follow-up indicates that you have made an error, go back to Step 1 and begin again.

Where We Are

In the first eight chapters, we dealt mainly with Steps 1, 2, and 3 in the decision-making process. We also gave some attention to Steps 4 and 5. In this chapter, we will work our way from Step 4 through Step 7. The last two chapters in the book are designed to help you with Steps 8 and 9.

Step 4 in the decision-making process says "evaluate." "Evaluate" means to judge. Whenever you judge anything you have to use standards. Every time you choose one thing over another you're using standards for judgment. When you choose milk instead of coffee, you're using standards. When you choose a movie instead of a game, you're using standards. When you choose to date only one person—or to break up— you're using standards. Maybe they're not very clear in your mind, but you are using standards just the same. You use standards all the time.

When you make your career choice, you will be using standards. The quality of those standards will affect the quality of your choice. You need good standards. A rubber yardstick or one with unclear markings won't let you measure accurately. So you should give a lot of thought to the standards you will use in judging occupations. Some of your standards will reflect your personal preferences. They will belong to you alone. But some things should be included in *everyone's* set of standards for choosing an occupation.

The Basic Standards

Actually, you've already seen these basic standards back in Chapter 5. On page 48 you read what a good occupational choice should provide for you. It should give you (1) adequate income, (2) security, (3) real pleasure from daily activities, (4) a feeling of importance, (5) some freedom on the job, and (6) an opportunity for personal growth. A good occupational choice will give you all of these things. These are the things that people really seek from their jobs. They can be used as basic standards for judging any occupation.

The Point System

With these things in mind, let's discuss some ways to judge occupations. You may evaluate occupations in two ways. You may use a point system to evaluate occupations one at a time. Or you may use a factor-by-factor system to evaluate occupations in groups.

First, let's discuss the point system. Look at Figure 6, below. It's called a "Point System Occupation Evaluation Sheet." When using the point system, you will use a form like this. You can make your own forms. You will need one for each occupation being considered.

POINT SYSTEM OCCUPATION EVALUATION SHEET Occupation: _____		Degree Codes Provided by the job: 5 = To a great extent 4 = To a large extent 3 = To an average extent 2 = To a low-average extent 1 = To a small extent	
Factors	**Degree**	**Multiplier**	**Weighted Points**
Adequate Income			
Security			
Pleasure from Daily Activities			
Feeling of Importance			
Freedom on the Job			
Opportunity for Personal Growth			
Other			
Other			
Other			
Other			
Total Unweighted Points: _____		**Total Weighted Points:** _____	

Figure 6   **Point System Occupation Evaluation Sheet**

To make a form, write the six basic standards (factors) on a piece of paper. Write them one below the other, down the left-hand side of the page. Below these six, add any other factors that are personally important to you. These might include such things as working conditions, location, opportunity to travel, and so forth.

Then, to the right of the six factors, make a vertical column. Label it "Degree." This column will help you estimate *how much* of each factor a given job will provide for you. For the moment, ignore the "Multiplier" and "Weighted Points" columns. We will talk about them soon. In the upper right-hand corner of your paper, write the "Degree Codes" shown in the upper right-hand corner of Figure 6.

Now take the first occupation on your list. Write the occupation's title on the top of your evaluation sheet. Then ask yourself, "To what extent, compared with all the occupations I am considering, will this occupation give me an Adequate Income?" Your answer should be based on all the information you can get. If your answer is "To a great extent," write a 5 in the Degree column on the Adequate Income line. If your answer is "To a large extent," write a 4 in the Degree column on the Adequate Income line. The number you write in the Degree column should be taken from the Degree Codes shown in the upper right-hand corner of your form. You may answer with a 5, 4, 3, 2, or 1, depending on the extent to which that occupation will provide you with an Adequate Income. The better the income, the higher the code number it should be given.

When you're finished with Income, move on to Security. Ask yourself, "To what extent, compared with all the occupations I am considering, will this occupation give me Security?" After careful thought, assign that occupation its proper number of points by writing a code number in the Degree column. When you've finished with Security, go on to Pleasure from Daily Activities. Follow the same careful judging process. Do this until you've finished the entire list of factors for the first occupation.

When you have filled in the Degree column for all factors, add up the points in that column. Write the total on the line for "Total Unweighted Points." The more points the occupation has, the higher you have rated it.

When you are done with the first occupation, take a new form. Go through the same process for the second occupation you are considering. Complete a form for each occupation on your list, using the same factors for all occupations. When you have done that, look at the Total Unweighted Points shown on each form. The occupations with the most points are the ones you should consider most seriously.

Before going on, stop and consider that your results could be faulty. There could be several reasons for this. You may have been hasty when choosing your Degree Codes. Or you may not have been careful when choosing your personal factors ("Other" on Figure 6). Your results will be faulty if your Degree Code selections were made based on guesswork rather than on valid information. If you don't have enough information to judge the factors on the form, you don't know enough about the occupation. Study it some more.

Multipliers

The system described above is a simple evaluation method. It works fine as long as all of the factors are equally important to you. But what if Income is twice as important to you as Security? Or if Security is three times as important as Opportunity for Personal Growth? How can such things be taken into account? What you do in such cases (this applies to many people) is to *weight* the factors according to their importance.

A weighted evaluation is a refinement of the point system. It's a little more complicated. But it deserves serious consideration because it is more precise than the basic system.

To use the weighted system, you give each factor a multiplier. Let's use our six original factors to show how it works. Look again at Figure 6. If you have not already done so, add Multiplier and Weighted Points columns to each occupation evaluation sheet you are using.

Now, suppose you decide that, *for you,* Security and a Feeling of Importance are equally important. Also, suppose that for you they are the least important of the six factors. Give each of them a 1 as a multiplier and write it in the Multiplier column.

Then suppose you decide that Adequate Income, Pleasure from Daily Activities, and Freedom on the Job are each twice as important as the previous two factors. Give each of these factors a 2 in the Multiplier column.

Finally, suppose you think Opportunity for Personal Growth is three times as important as the first two factors. Its multiplier, then, should be 3.

It's up to you to decide on the multiplier for each factor. The "supposes" in the previous paragraphs may not be true for you at all. Only when you've decided how you really feel should you write numbers down in the Multiplier column on the sheet. Each factor may have a different number for a multiplier. You can even use decimals if they are appropriate.

Once you have carefully determined and recorded your multipliers, you are ready to use them. Multipliers are simple to use. Just multiply the number written in the Degree column for each factor by the value of its multiplier. For example, suppose you wrote a 3 in the Degree column for Adequate Income. If you gave Adequate Income a multiplier of 2, then the weighted points for Adequate Income would be 6. Fill in the blank accordingly. To get the Total Weighted Points for an occupation, just add the weighted points for each of its factors. To compare different occupations, compare their Total Weighted Points. The greater the Total, the higher the rating.

By this system you rate all factors for one occupation, and arrive at a weighted score for it. Then you rate all factors for each of the succeeding occupations on your list and arrive at weighted scores for them. Then you compare the point totals.

Another way to evaluate occupations is to use the factor-by-factor system. This method is a little more complex. It may, however, permit you to make sharper comparisons.

The Factor-by-Factor System

In this system you rate all occupations on your list one factor at a time. Assume that there are four occupations on your list. First, you rate all four occupations for Adequate Income. Then you rate all four for Security. Then you rate all of them for Pleasure from Daily Activities. You proceed like this until you have evaluated all jobs for all factors. Then you use multipliers if you wish, add up totals, and compare as before.

Look at Figure 7 on the next page. It is a model of a form to use when using this factor-by-factor system. On the point system sheet, you worked from top to bottom. On this sheet you work across the page, in a line.

The numbers in the upper right corner of Figure 7 are the same codes as in Figure 6. They help you rate the extent to which you believe each job will provide you with the various factors. So after you have written in the name of Job 1 on your list, pick its proper Degree Code for Adequate Income. Write the code number in the Degree column for Job 1. Then enter the proper code number for Job 2's Adequate Income factor. Continue rating Adequate Income for each job across the page. Then move down one line and do the same thing for each job's Security factor. Proceed down the page until all factors for all jobs have been rated. Then total and compare the unweighted points for each job.

If you want to weight your evaluations, write an appropriate multiplier in each factor's Multiplier column. Then multiply, fill in the Weighted Points columns, and add up the totals as you did in the point system.

FACTOR-BY-FACTOR OCCUPATION EVALUATION SHEET

Degree Codes

Provided by the job:

5 = To a great extent
4 = To a large extent
3 = To an average extent
2 = To a low-average extent
1 = To a small extent

Factors	Multiplier	JOB 1 Title:		JOB 2 Title:		JOB 3 Title:		JOB 4 Title:	
		Degree	Weighted Points	Degree	Weighted Points	Degree	Weighted Points	Degree	Weighted Points
Adequate Income									
Security									
Pleasure from Daily Activities									
Feeling of Importance									
Freedom on the Job									
Opportunity for Personal Growth									
Other									
Other									
Other									
Other									
	Total Unweighted Points	Total Weighted Points	Total Unweighted Points	Total Weighted Points	Total Unweighted Points	Total Weighted Points	Total Unweighted Points	Total Weighted Points

Figure 7 **Factor-by-Factor Occupation Evaluation Sheet**

Don't be discouraged by the apparent complexity of this system. It has the important advantage of letting you concentrate on one factor at a time. This helps you get your analysis into very sharp focus.

You might want to compare the two methods. To do this you would take two or three occupations and evaluate each of them both ways. Then use the method you prefer for the remaining occupations on your list. Or if you want to double-check yourself, you could evaluate all occupations both ways. Then you could compare the results and figure out the reasons for any differences that occur.

What We've Done

In this chapter, you have seen some systems for using all the ideas we have considered. This is where you put it all together.

Think about those Occupation Evaluation Sheets. In order to know what ratings to give to Adequate Income, Security, and Freedom on the Job, you have to know occupations and the world of work. If you don't have this information, you simply cannot make Degree assignments in an intelligent way. That's why occupations and the world of work were discussed in Chapters 5, 6, and 7. Chapter 7 even shows you where to go for more information if you need it.

In order to know what ratings to give to Pleasure from Daily Activities, Feeling of Importance, and Opportunity for Personal Growth, you have to know yourself. That's why we discussed human needs in Chapter 3 and personality types in Chapter 4. Your occupation should bring you pleasure, while at the same time meeting your other needs. To find that occupation, your Adult needs to be in control. This was discussed in Chapter 2. As you can see, Occupation Evaluation Sheets are indeed based on all the ideas contained in the previous chapters.

Back in Chapter 1, you read about several theories of occupational choice. All of them help explain how people choose their careers. Each theory tells a little about you, your alternatives, and your problems. Now you should understand that process. If you don't, take another look at Chapter 1. Understanding the process can help you reach a sound conclusion.

Wait a Minute

Now wait a minute. Have you thrown up your hands, saying "Your plan is too complicated," or "It is too much bother"? If so, think again about the importance of this decision. Except for choosing a spouse, this may be the most important decision you will ever make. It's worth all the thought and effort you can give it.

Besides, these systems really are not hard to use. Try them. They will make you think, but you will catch on quickly. More importantly, these systems will help guide you toward a better life.

QUESTIONS FOR THOUGHT AND DISCUSSION

1. What is the first step in the decision-making process?

2. What is a "standard"? What are standards used for? Name three of your personal standards.

3. According to this chapter, a good occupation will give you at least six important things. What are they? Rank them according to their importance to you. How much more important to you is the first one than the last?

4. Explain the purpose of the Multiplier on the Occupation Evaluation Sheets. Will you be using it to help evaluate occupations? Why or why not?

5. Which is the better approach: (a) evaluating occupations one at a time, or (b) evaluating them in groups, factor by factor? Why?

6. Is it really worth the effort to evaluate occupations in detail, point by point? Why or why not? Who will be the loser if you don't make the effort?

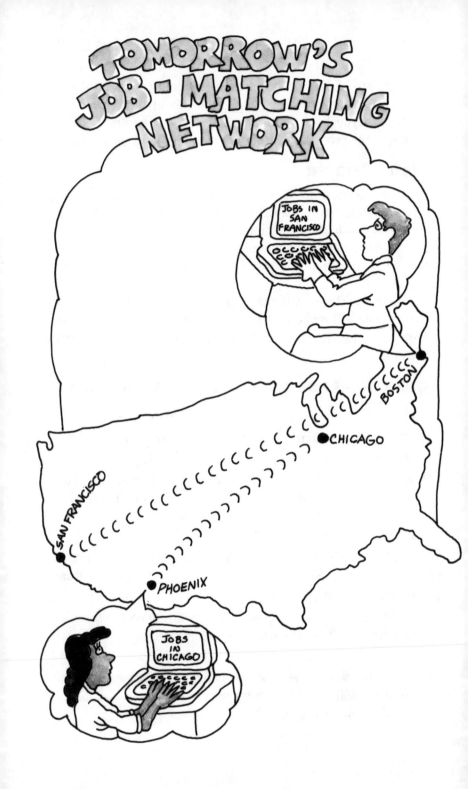

Finding the Right Position

Acting on a good idea is better than just having a good idea.

It is possible that you can spend a great deal of time and effort choosing your occupation, and still be disappointed. This can happen if you go to work in the wrong organization. Some occupations can be found in many kinds of organizations. For example, business, professional, and government organizations employ engineers, accountants, clerks, programmers, and secretaries. If your skills can be used in many different places, you must try to find the best possible place in which to use them.

This is not easy. It's a big country, and you're going to need help in your search. Even with help, you never can be sure that you have found the best position. But with help, you'll find a better position than you would if you try to find it by yourself.

Tomorrow It Will Be Easier

Probably you will see the day when there will be a huge, nationwide computer network to match people with jobs. Employers all over the country will plug data about their jobs into the system. Job seekers from every state will plug information about themselves into the same system. A computer will find the best match of persons with jobs. Then the computer will inform the interested parties.

103

Fantastic? Well, it's coming. By using this network, a young man in Boston could locate jobs suitable for him in San Francisco. The process would take only minutes. A young woman in Phoenix who wanted to work in Chicago could quickly find out what jobs existed for her there. An employer in Miami could select qualified applicants from all over the country for a job needing to be filled. Such a system could be a great help in matching people and jobs.

Already there are several systems of this kind operating in the United States. In California, a job-matching system called LINCS (Labor Inventory Communication System) connects local offices of the state employment service. It is used to place managerial, technical, and professional workers. There is another system connecting employment service offices in Madison, Wisconsin. It's called ESOPS (Employment Service On-Line Placement System), and it covers all kinds of jobs. In Utah there is the Utah Job-Matching System. It has been in operation since 1968. This system is said to serve more than 90% of the state's population. In New York City there is the AMDS (Area Manpower Data System). It connects all the city's employment service offices. There are other systems as well.

So we have a start on computerized job-matching. Keep an eye on new developments in that field. It will grow gradually, but it is on the way.

How About Today?

We don't have a fully developed nationwide computerized job-matching system today. So what does a person like you do? You do the next best thing. You use all the help that is available now. Actually, you have a lot going for you. If your idea of a job search is reading ads in the local newspaper and setting out on foot, you had better think again.

Job-search assistance facilities vary from city to city. But even if they were the same everywhere, people probably would not agree on one best way of looking for a job. So I won't suggest one best way. Instead, this chapter will show you some of the places you can go for help and information. These places include your school, people who are working, published information, and employment agencies. Let's look at each of them in more detail.

Help from Your School

If your school has a placement officer, talk with that person. The placement officer should be the best-informed individual in the entire school on jobs and job markets. Explain what you're looking for. The placement officer will help you find it. If you aren't clear on which of several jobs would be best for you, discuss them. Study the pamphlets in the placement office. Read the bulletin board. Your school placement office is the main contact point between the school and the world of jobs. Don't fail to use it.

Talk with your teachers. Often teachers have contacts that placement officers don't have. Good teachers know what is happening in the community. Sometimes a teacher can make one phone call that can change your life. Teachers of vocational courses are especially likely to keep up to date on job information.

Talk to the other students in your class. Find out if there are any occupations in which several of you share an interest. Then, with the list of occupations in hand, talk to a teacher or guidance counselor. Ask him or her to invite guest speakers to talk to the class about those jobs.

If your school has an annual job fair, where students can talk with people sent by different companies, attend it. Ask these representatives for information. If your school offers a course or unit on careers, take it. Sometimes recruiters go to schools to talk with graduating seniors. If they come to your school, set up appointments with them. These people can give you good information. They also can help you develop your interviewing skills.

Help from Working People

Talk with your friends. Find out what they've learned. Talk with your parents. Talk with the parents of your friends. Suppose you're seeking a job as a computer programmer. If you have a friend whose parent works with computers, talk with that person. He or she may be able to give you information you could not get elsewhere.

The same holds true no matter what job you are seeking. Talk with people who do that kind of work. If they happen to be people you know, so much the better.

Help from Published Information

The want-ad sections of newspapers are popular places to look for job information. Most job seekers are wise to read the papers. But don't restrict yourself to your local papers. Read as many papers as you can. Many libraries have newspapers from all over the country.

An excellent source of information for college students is the *College Placement Annual*.[1] This three-volume 800-page publication comes out every year. It is available at college placement offices. It contains thousands of job opportunities. The listings are indexed by occupation and by the location of employers throughout the nation and overseas. If you're not familiar with this publication, find out about it and study it. It is filled with valuable information.

Other excellent sources of job information are the trade and professional journals. Almost every occupation has at least one special magazine that is read by people working in that field. For example, there are *The Carpenter, Advertising Age, The Personnel Administrator,* and *Aviation Week*. Many such publications have employment sections in the back. The jobs listed there often are very good ones. They are jobs of interest only to people who read that kind of publication. These jobs might not be advertised anywhere else. These publications serve as an insider's employment service.

So read the professional or trade publications for occupations that interest you. You'll find many of them in your library. They may help you find a job. They also contain up-to-date information about trades and professions. In fact, these journals provide one of the major ways in which people keep up to date in their fields. You can be sure that your doctor reads medical journals.

The federal government advertises jobs in bulletins sent to post offices across the country. If you are interested in working for the U.S. government, first check at your local post office. Look at the announcements on the bulletin boards. Ask about new bulletins that may not yet be posted.

Sending Letters and Résumés

Thousands of the best jobs are filled without any advertising at all. So many people apply for them that companies don't have to advertise. If you would like to work for a particular organization, write and tell them so. Send them a letter saying what kind of job you want. Tell them what you can do and why you want to work for them. Ask for an interview. Your librarian and placement officer can help you find addresses. There are books that list the addresses of companies all over the country.

You will need to prepare another document to go with your letter. You should draw up a *résumé*. A résumé is a short summary of your education and work experience. If you have a copy of the *College Placement Annual,* look at the sample résumé there. If you don't have a copy, ask for help in finding another example. Make your résumé personal and make it one page, or two at most. Remember to send *both* a letter and a résumé to potential employers.

Don't be afraid to send out letters and résumés. While many of them may not bring results, some of them will. This is an excellent way of making employers know that you exist. They cannot hire you if they don't know that you exist. Send out many letters. Students often send out fifty or more. The more you send out, the better your chances of finding a job that suits you.

Employment Agencies

Employment agencies are special organizations that help people find jobs. There are two kinds of employment agencies—public and private. Public agencies are run by the government. They provide free service to the public. Private agencies are run by individuals or companies. Since they work for profit, they charge fees for their services. First we will look at public employment agencies.

Public Employment Agencies   Public employment agencies also are called *state employment offices.* They have two main tasks: helping people find jobs and handling unemployment compensation for people who are out of work. Probably you will find your state employment office a rather busy place.

State employment offices provide three services for job seekers: counseling, testing, and referral. If you're not sure of your abilities, these offices can give you tests that will help you discover them. If you need counseling on what kind of job to take, a counselor will be glad to talk with you. After it's clear what you can and want to do, contacts can be made with employers. They will interview you, and perhaps they will give you a job.

Most state employment offices place people in nearby jobs. But these offices do have contact with other offices in your city and in other cities. So it is possible that they could help you find a job some distance from your home.

Private Employment Agencies   Private employment agencies often are not quite as busy as public agencies. They have nothing to do with unemployment compensation. And since they charge a fee for their service, they give a good deal

of attention to each job seeker. Their fees vary, but it is common for the fee to be about half of one month's pay. So if a private agency places you in a job paying $1,000 a month, the fee might be about $500. Bear in mind, though, that this is just a rough rule of thumb.

Sometimes the fee is paid by the employer. Sometimes it is paid by the applicant. Sometimes it is split, depending on the job. Naturally you should check this before being placed in a job by a private employment agency.

Private agencies also test, counsel, and refer their clients. Sometimes they specialize in certain kinds of jobs, such as sales, clerical, or technical occupations. Often they have contacts with private employment agencies in other cities. In fact, we now have several nationwide private employment-agency chains.

Why would anyone pay for assistance when free help is available from state employment offices? Basically it is because private agencies often give more attention to each person. They also are able to do certain things that state employment offices usually don't emphasize. For example, they give help to people who *are* working, but who want to find better jobs.

Labor Unions

Many labor unions help their members get jobs. This is especially true of the "craft" unions—those of carpenters, plumbers, and electricians, for example. In some industries, like construction and shipping, a lot of job placement is done through unions. Some unions, with help from employers, conduct apprenticeship programs. In these programs, people learn the skills needed in particular trades.

There are hundreds of apprenticeable occupations. Industries such as electronics, construction, health care, and service offer apprenticeships. The U.S. Department of Labor, through local Bureaus of Apprenticeship and Training, provides a great deal of information on apprenticeships. Your state's Apprenticeship Agency also is a good source of information on these training programs.

A Word of Warning

By now it should be clear that there are many sources of help for job seekers. Most employment agencies are happy, even eager, to have you take a job to which they've sent you. If you take it, they feel they have accomplished their goal. In the case of a private employment agency, it has earned its fee.

However, you would be wise to avoid jumping at the first job that comes along. It could be that the first opportunity is right for you. This is especially true if both you and the job have been well screened. But you're making a mistake if you assume that this is just what has happened. Especially when jobs are plentiful, you should look before you leap. Take your time. Check several jobs. The best job you'll ever find probably is not the first one that comes along.

Even if jobs are hard to find, you should check on a company before you decide to work for it. A little checking may help you avoid a big mistake.

Checking on Companies

Remember that organizations are made up of people. Like people, organizations differ. Company A may be quite different from Company B. Unless you expect to be self-employed, you're not going to *just* be a computer programmer, for example. You're going to be a computer programmer working for some organization. What that organization is can make a big difference in your life.

Some firms allow employees to dress casually. Others require formal business dress. Some have a history of trouble with unions. Some have no connection with unions. Some are quick to lay people off. Others have never had a layoff. Some make good products. Others turn out inferior products. Some are run like dictatorships; others aren't. Some treat employees like members of a family; others don't. Some are secretive; others are open. Some have excellent benefit programs; others don't. Some grow; others stagnate. Some fail. Yes indeed, there are all kinds of companies.

The point is this: You are not just applying for a job. You are applying for a job *with a specific company*. You need to learn as much as possible about that firm before you invest part of your life in it. After all, the firm will learn a lot about you before it invests in you. The bare facts about job duties and pay are important. But other information on the company is important, too.

Read about the companies before you go on interviews. Ask your librarian for books like *Moody's*[2] and *Standard and Poor's*.[3] Ask for other information on firms that interest you. Talk with people who work at various firms. Find out how each one treats its employees.

Ask questions in interviews. *Ask first about the job.* Find out exactly what it is. Investigate your chances for promotion. Then talk about pay and working hours, about insurance and other benefits. Most interviewers will be honest with you if you are sincere. But remember that the interviewer is looking out for the company. You have to look out for yourself.

So whatever you do, check companies out. It pays to do this before your interview. But certainly you should check on a firm thoroughly before you go to work for it. Your research may reassure you about the firm. Or what you discover may turn your warning lights on. To make a good decision, you need to have the facts.

Getting the Most Out of Your Interview

A job interview should be a two-way street. Information should flow in both directions—to you and from you. Go in as relaxed as possible, looking neat and clean. Arm yourself with the questions you want answered. Take notes with you if you'd like. Don't be afraid to take notes while you're there.

Try to be open and honest, and hope that your interviewer will be the same. But remember that both you and the interviewer may put on "masks" or "false fronts." You may do this to make yourself look as good as possible. And yes, your interviewer may do it for the same reason.

Because of this, the flow of information in a job interview may be filtered. Statements cannot always be taken as the whole truth. Your interviewer won't lie to you. He or she may, however, put on the firm's best face. Unpleasant information may be left out of the discussion. This will happen especially if there's interest in you. So be careful. Ask questions, and take notes.

It's hard to say who will be interviewing you. In a big firm, the first step probably will be an interview with a personnel worker. In a small firm your interview may be with the owner or with the person who would be your boss. The person you really need to talk with is the person who would be your direct supervisor.

If you're applying at a large company, a personnel worker may set up an interview with your potential supervisor. If this is done, fine. If not, and the firm seems interested in you, ask for a chance to talk with the person to whom you'd report. It's not asking too much. Any good company will respect you for asking.

Talk with your potential superior about the job. Also try to size him or her up as a person. After all, if you get the job, your boss will hold the key to your future. This will be explained more fully in the next chapter. For now, let's just say that you really need to meet your immediate superior. It is also a good idea to see the place where you would be working. Try to meet some of the people who would be working with you. They can heavily influence your happiness on the job.

In short, don't just sit through an interview answering questions. Be courteous, but remember you are there to get information as well as to give it. You are putting your future on the line. Any company you really want to work for will go out of its way to give you all the information you need.

Some companies will ask you to complete application forms. These forms are designed to obtain information about your work experience and job qualifications. Be sure to fill in all the blanks on the forms, and to do it as neatly as you can. You may be asked for your social security number, so take your card and other identification with you.

Often, companies ask applicants to take physical exams or other tests. You may have to take an aptitude test or a test of the hands-on skills the job requires. Try to relax during these tests. Remember, the other applicants have to take the tests too, so you're in good company.

Application blanks, physical exams, tests—these all provide just a one-way flow of information, from you to the company. If the company requires them, do them. Be as complete, neat, and accurate as you can be. But remember that your chance to get information is in the interviews. Plan ahead. Write down the things you want to know. Be sure to get that information before you take the job.

Summing It Up

It was said earlier that making a good career choice requires a wide search of occupations. Now we are saying that once you have chosen an occupation, you have to make a second search. You have to search for the best place at which to work. This second search is almost as important as the first.

Think back to Figure 5 in Chapter 8. It showed you in the middle of a circle with the world of occupations all around. When you're searching for the right career, you are in a situation like that. Later, when you're searching for the right job, you are right back in the middle again. Once again you must make a search.

So do yourself a favor. Make a good search. Use all the help that is available. Find out what is really there. Find out what you'd be getting into before you commit yourself. Always investigate before you take a job. And make interviews work for you.

QUESTIONS FOR THOUGHT AND DISCUSSION

1. What information should be included in a résumé? How should that information be organized in order to be most effective?

2. Why should you send both a letter and a résumé to potential employers?

3. What are the two major duties of a public employment agency?

4. How does a private employment agency differ from a public employment office? What are the advantages and disadvantages of the two types of agencies?

5. Why is it important to check out a firm before going to work for it? What kinds of information about the firm should you seek?

6. What questions should you ask when interviewing for a job? Which questions should come first? Which should come later? Why? HINT: If you want to make a good impression, when should you ask about pay and vacations?

7. Is it really true that both applicants and interviewers may "wear masks" during job interviews? Why is this? Does it help or hinder good job placements?

8. In what ways do companies differ from one another? Do companies really have "personalities"? If so, is it important for a person to work for a firm whose "personality" matches his or her own? Why?

11 Making a Living

*Find pleasure in your work
or you will not find pleasure.*

When a person takes a job, he or she begins some important relationships with an employer and with fellow employees. These relationships involve more than many people seem to think. Taking a job is not simply a matter of selling a certain amount of time or skill for money. Taking a job means entering a way of life. Your job occupies more of your time than any other activity. You spend most of your waking hours working, getting ready for work, and going to and from work. Because of this, it can become the center of your life.

When people take new jobs, they usually try very hard to fit in. They look for clues about acting, dressing, and talking. They obey the leader. They follow the group's code and try to become accepted members of the group. If they are successful, they get more than just money in return for their work. They also receive social payoffs from the group. These social payoffs may go a long way toward satisfying the needs in the middle of their need pyramids. These are the needs for safety, belongingness, and esteem.

A price must be paid to satisfy these needs. The price requires a person to go beyond just doing the job. It means giving social rewards to fellow workers. A person has to give to fellow workers the same things he or she hopes to receive: safety, belongingness, and esteem. While these social relationships do help to satisfy deep human needs, they also make us conform to social expectations.

So a job has both economic and social aspects. A person's employer expects an *economic* payoff (profit) from the employee's services. The employee expects an economic payoff in the form of a decent wage. A person's co-workers expect a *social* payoff from him or her, and the same is expected in return. Both kinds of payoffs must flow in both directions. Otherwise, the employment relationship will not succeed.

When an employment relationship breaks down, the cause is more often social than economic. One of the reasons for this is that it's difficult to discover the social climate of a job until you are in it. It is easy to get economic facts about a job before you take it. The interviewer can tell you about wages, insurance, vacations, and other benefits. You can be told about working hours, overtime, and payday. You can be given a good idea of the work that you'll be doing. But it's hard to know how you will get along with your co-workers and with your boss.

Most people walk into a new job "cold." They know very little about their co-workers and their bosses. They are a little worried about how they'll fit in. Usually they try hard to become accepted. Sometimes things work out, and sometimes they don't. If things work out—fine. The new employee will be content and do good work. If things don't work out, the problem will lie in the employee's relationship with (1) the boss, (2) the co-workers, or (3) the work itself. Let's take a closer look at each of these relationships.

The Boss

The boss is a key figure in any person's life. He or she is a source of rewards and punishments. This person tells you what to do, and it is he or she who measures your success. A businessman, when asked for his definition of success, gave the following: "Success is whatever the boss thinks it is." That may be stretching it a bit, but there is a lot of truth in the man's remark.

So the boss is your judge. He or she also is a shaper of people. It is very likely that you will be changed by the beliefs and behavior of your boss. The boss often is not aware of his or her influence, especially upon younger workers. Yet this person may turn out to be a key figure in a new employee's total life. Why? Because the first boss introduces a person to the world of work. These first impressions tend to last.

Theories X and Y Dr. Douglas McGregor wrote an excellent book called *The Human Side of Enterprise.*[1] This book discusses the effect of a boss's attitudes upon his or her workers. Different bosses have differing attitudes. McGregor wrote that *some* bosses think the average worker is lazy, stupid, lacking in ambition, and really doesn't care about the company. He gave a name to this set of ideas. He called it "Theory X."

McGregor stated that *other* bosses share a different set of ideas about the average worker. He called this set of ideas "Theory Y." It is almost the opposite of Theory X. A boss who believes in Theory Y feels that the average worker is bright, willing to work, has lots of ambition, and does care about the company.

Both theories are extreme, and probably most bosses are somewhere in the middle. Still, McGregor's book suggests that every boss has a basic tendency toward believing in either Theory X or Theory Y. Some bosses take an optimistic view of the average worker. Others tend to be pessimistic.

"That's interesting," you say, "but so what?" Well, McGregor made a study of this. He found that no matter what a boss believes, he or she can prove the point. If one boss believes in Theory X, he or she can prove it. If another boss believes in Theory Y, he or she can prove that.

How can a boss prove that he or she is right? Simply by pointing to his or her workers. If one boss believes that workers are lazy and stupid and don't care—that's the way his or her people are. And if another boss believes that workers are bright, ambitious, and willing to work—that's the way his or her people are. Both theories seem to be self-fulfilling.

McGregor then asked some embarrassing questions, at least as far as Theory X bosses were concerned. He said, "Well, it seems that you are right. Your employees are as you said they would be. But tell me, how did they get that way? Were they born lazy? Did they learn to have no ambition at their mothers' knees? Did their education make them stupid? Or did something happen to them on the job?"

To make a long story short, McGregor concluded that the average worker is just that—average. A worker comes into a company as an average person and is somewhat moldable. He or she can be shaped in any number of directions. The boss is a shaper. If the boss believes that workers are lazy, stupid, and have no ambition, he or she will treat them accordingly. And after being treated in this way over a period of time, the workers will tend to become exactly what the boss expected them to be from the beginning.

If another boss has an optimistic opinion of the average worker, this will show up in the boss's behavior. His or her workers will be treated as though they were bright, ambitious, and willing to work. And in treating them that way, the boss will be shaping their behavior and their beliefs about them-selves. They too will become what the boss expected from the beginning.

Well, this is just a theory and not everyone believes in it. Theory Y managers believe in it. Many college professors believe in it. But Theory X managers do not believe in it. You can believe whatever you want about it. My conclusion is that there is something to this theory. People are shaped by others in authority over them—parents, teachers, bosses. You can't choose your parents, and sometimes you can't choose your teachers. But often you can choose your boss.

Give it some thought. What is going to happen to you if you work eight hours a day, five days a week for a boss who

Theory X

Theory Y

treats you as if you were stupid? Will you think well of yourself? Will you develop your skills? Will you try to get ahead? Will you enjoy your work? You know very well what will happen.

In a way, a Theory X boss makes "turtles" out of his or her workers. The workers are driven into their shells. They spend much of their time just trying to defend themselves. And like the turtle, while they're in their shells they're not moving ahead.

Due largely to education, bosses' and employees' attitudes are getting better. There are fewer Theory X bosses now. But there are still plenty of them out there in the world of work. If you should find yourself working for a Theory X boss, you will have a serious problem. You might want to consider quitting the company. It's possible that you could change the boss. It's more likely, however, that he or she will change you. Would you want to be changed in that way? You may never have to face this problem, but it could happen.

Fellow Workers

When you really stop to think about it, you will find that most of your social payoffs in life come from just a few people. These people belong to your "reference groups." These might be family, a few close friends, a club or two, a church perhaps— and fellow workers on the job. That's just about it in most cases. You can see from this that your co-workers are important figures in your life, and vice versa. You give—or deny— each other social payoffs that are vital to satisfying basic needs.

In the process, you tend to conform to the expectations of others in your reference groups. You become more like them, and they become more like you. As time goes on, you think and act more and more like others in your occupation. You take on certain qualities that tend to be shared by people in your occupation.

Some experts go so far as to say that they can predict your general behavior, without ever seeing you, if someone will tell them about your reference groups. This may be a little extreme, for there are great differences among people. Still, the influence of reference groups cannot be denied.

So a person doesn't just work and then go home. A worker's job relationships are brought home. They help to shape the person, on and off the job. Of course, every person plays a number of different roles—family member, voter, taxpayer, consumer, and so forth. But the role of "worker at such and such a job" may be the most basic role of all. People seldom escape the influence of their jobs and the people with whom they work.

So try to get along with your co-workers. Build them up, don't put them down. You need each other and can help each other. We usually get back from others pretty much what we give out.

The Work Itself

For a long time, we didn't realize how important it was for a person to have a job that had variety, interest, and challenge. Managers broke jobs down into smaller and smaller parts. Finally, what was left were simple tasks that almost anyone could learn in a few hours. We didn't seem to realize that people get feelings of importance from their work.

We now know that people do get feelings of importance from their work. We know that if someone *thinks* a job is small and low, he or she is likely to feel small and low doing it. We know that many people want to move up to bigger jobs. They want to move on to more challenging and more important work. Not everyone wants to advance, but most people do. Yet whatever our jobs, most of us feel entitled to some prestige from the kind of work we do.

A newspaper item mentioned a production worker who often was absent, especially on Fridays. He was asked, "Why do you so often skip work on Fridays? Why do you work only four days?" His answer was, "Because I don't earn enough to live on in three days." Obviously, this man hated his job. Nobody knows how many workers feel that way. It's tragic, however, that even one does.

But before we go too far, let's back up a little. A job that is dull and boring to one person might be a challenge for another. Employers have recognized this. They try to hire people whose attitudes are ideally suited to the jobs available. Also, many employers are trying to enlarge boring jobs to make them more interesting.

So a job isn't by nature dull and low. It is like this only in somebody's opinion. The key is to get yourself a job that is not dull and low for you. Remember, too, that a job that is challenging today may become boring tomorrow, after you have mastered it. This is another reason why people keep changing jobs. The job to get is the job that's right for you *at this time.*

Later, if you do your work well, you may move up. People learn and grow in their jobs, not just in school. Someone interested in health services, for example, might begin working as an ambulance attendant. With experience and training, this person might move up to lab work. One day, he or she might become a technician. With further training and experience, this person might become a lab supervisor. Later, he or she might even decide to study medicine. Careers develop as people develop.

Management Attitudes: The Old Days

There was a time in this country when many employers cared very little about their workers. This was true especially of employers of unskilled workers. People were hired and fired on the spot. On the job, they often were treated like animals. Young children tended machines in the mills. Women worked in firetrap sweatshops. For men, it was survival of the fittest. When a nation is growing, some groups often are taken advantage of in the process. The ordinary working people have had rough times in the past, even in America.

Gradually, though, laws that reduced child labor were enacted. Children were allowed to go to school instead of working. Safety laws were passed. The eight-hour day became standard, and minimum wages were established. People became better educated. New machines took heavy burdens off the backs of human beings. Labor unions became powerful. Managers became more considerate—partly because they had to, and partly because they learned that people who are treated better will work better.

There came a time when managers felt they had to do something about the jobs that nobody wanted to do. These were jobs that *everyone* thought were dull and low. At first, managers thought they could pay more money to the people who did the boring work, or improve the working conditions of those people. This helped a little. Workers and their unions began to accept and even demand these things.

But the hard fact was that higher pay and better working conditions didn't make the work itself more interesting. A person knows when a job is dull and low for him or her. Nothing but a change in the work itself is going to satisfy that person. No matter what the pay, there is still no pride to be found in a job you consider dull and low.

Management Attitudes: Human Relations

Some firms decided to try a new approach. It came to be called the "Human Relations" movement. The immediate goal of this movement was to make employees happy. In the long run, companies wanted to improve productivity. But they thought that if they could first make the workers happy through good human relations, the workers would be more productive. So the managers smiled more and gave out more praise.

The idea could be sketched like this:

Human Relations

Leadership ⟶ Happiness ⟶ Productivity

This was a big improvement over the sweatshops. But the problem of a worker's not getting a feeling of importance from a dull job was not solved. Boring work was still boring work.

Management Attitudes: Human Resources

Today companies are trying another idea. It is called "Human Resources." Productivity is still the goal of employers. While they're still trying to be nice to workers, they now feel that workers won't be happy until they are productive. The new idea suggests that workers should be well trained, well equipped, and given more job responsibility. Simple jobs are being enlarged. Workers are allowed to do more of their own planning and inspection. In short, workers are being given more authority and responsibility. Managers believe that if workers feel responsible and face more challenges, they will do better work. Also, they will get a feeling of importance from what they do.

The human resources idea could be sketched like this:

Human Resources

Leadership ⟶ Productivity ⟶ Happiness

No one knows how successful this approach will be. Probably it is not the final answer. But many managers now recognize the worker's need to feel important. They are trying to do something about it. We are getting more and more evidence that job satisfaction comes not from conditions around the job, but from the work itself.

We're dealing here with needs that are very high on our need pyramids. These are the needs for self-esteem and self-actualization. We may be able to fool other people, but it's harder to fool ourselves. We know whether our work deserves respect. We know whether we're really growing toward our full potential.

If our work is worthy and is helping us grow, we know it. Our highest needs are being filled. But if we're just working along in a job that has become routine, we're not growing. We're having to settle for satisfying needs lower down on the pyramid. That is not where most of us want to be.

In Conclusion

It was not so long ago when earning a living consumed almost all of a person's life. Men often began working as children and continued working until they got sick or crippled or until they died. They worked six, maybe seven days a week and 12 or more hours a day. They worked extremely hard. Women in the work force at this time had terrible conditions, too.

People had large families because parents needed all the hands they could get just to earn a living. If a worker got sick or ran into misfortune, there was nowhere to turn but to family, friends, or neighbors. Most people were poor. Working people had no sick leave or vacations. Many had not had the benefit of an education. As a result, they didn't know much about what was going on in the world around them. Life was short, it was restricted, and it was hard.

Life still can be hard, although in a psychological rather than a physical way. Work today is usually less physical and more mental. There is more public assistance for the needy. We live longer now, and have smaller families. Our working lives are getting shorter. We know more, and we travel more. In a very real way, education, electronics, and jet planes have set us free. We still have to work, and we still have worries. But many of us are no longer trapped and consumed by the sheer necessity of just making a living.

No one would say that life in America today is perfect. We still have ignorance, disease, wars, poverty, and discrimination. Overcrowding and pollution sometimes seem to be getting worse. Employers and politicians worry about the economy and the international balance of trade. But in spite of it all, life for the ordinary worker is getting better. Stories about the "good old days" are mostly myths and fairy tales.

As you go out into the world, you'll be standing on the shoulders of all the people who have gone before. You are inheriting the earth, and one day you will pass it on. As you put yourself into the stream and flow of people and their works, you'll find that people, with all their sweat and striving, have done much good. You, too, can do much good. There is much to be done.

But to do the most good, for yourself and for the world, you must apply yourself where you can produce the best results. Helping you find that place is what this book is all about.

QUESTIONS FOR THOUGHT AND DISCUSSION

1. It is claimed in this chapter that an employee is shaped in important ways by his or her boss. Do you believe this? If so, in what ways are employees shaped by bosses? If not, why do you doubt it?

2. What are the differences between Theories X and Y? Would you rather work for a Theory X boss or for a Theory Y boss? Why?

3. What is a "reference group"? Name three of your most important reference groups. In what ways are you influenced by them? Do you influence the other members of these groups in return? How?

4. Are some jobs dull and low? If so, what makes them that way? Could a job that is not dull and low for you now someday become that way for you? Can you give an example of this?

5. If careers develop as people develop, why is it important that the first step you take in choosing an occupation be a good one?

6. What is the difference, if any, between "Human Relations" and "Human Resources"? Do workers produce well because they are happy? Or are they happy because they produce well? Or is there no connection between happiness and productivity?

7. Are people's working lives really better today than they used to be? Give some examples to support your point of view.

Bibliography

References Cited in This Book

Chapter 1
Page 3

1. Anne Roe, *The Psychology of Occupations* (1956; reprint ed., Salem, N.Y.: Ayer Co., 1977).

Page 3

2. Donald E. Super, *The Psychology of Careers: An Introduction to Vocational Development* (New York: Harper & Row, 1957).

Page 4

3. John L. Holland, *Making Vocational Choices: A Theory of Careers* (Englewood Cliffs, N. J.: Prentice-Hall, 1973).

Page 5

4. Eli Ginzberg and others, *Occupational Choice: An Approach to a General Theory* (New York: Columbia University Press, 1951).

Chapter 2
Page 11

1. Thomas A. Harris, *I'm OK—You're OK: A Practical Guide to Transactional Analysis* (1969; paperback ed., New York: Avon Books, 1982).

Chapter 3
Page 19

1. This theory is discussed in many places, but most experts credit Abraham Maslow as the major originator. Abraham H. Maslow, ed., *Motivation and Personality,* 2nd ed. (New York: Harper & Row, 1970).

Chapter 5
Page 43

1. For a more complete discussion, see Jack L. Rettig, "On the Meaning of Work," *Performance and Instruction,* June, 1982.

Chapter 6
Page 51

1. U.S. Department of Labor, Bureau of Labor Statistics, *Monthly Labor Review* (Washington, D.C.: U.S. Government Printing Office).

Chapter 7
Page 67

1. U.S. Department of Labor, Bureau of Labor Statistics, *Dictionary of Occupational Titles,* 4th ed. (Washington, D.C.: U.S. Government Printing Office, 1977).

Page 70

2. U.S. Department of Labor, Bureau of Labor Statistics, *Occupational Outlook Handbook,* 1984–85 ed. (Washington, D.C.: U.S. Government Printing Office, 1984).

Page 71

3. U.S. Department of Labor, Bureau of Labor Statistics, *Occupational Outlook Quarterly* (Washington, D.C.: U.S. Government Printing Office).

Page 74

4. Richard N. Bolles, *What Color Is Your Parachute?* (Berkeley, Calif.: Ten-Speed Press, 1979).

Page 74

5. Anna Mae Walsh Burke, *What Do You Want to Be Now That You're All Grown Up?* (Englewood Cliffs, N. J.: Prentice-Hall, 1982).

Page 74

6. Gail Sheehy, *Passages: Predictable Crises of Adult Life* (New York: E.P. Dutton, 1976).

Page 74

7. Studs Terkel, *Working* (New York: Pantheon Books, 1974).

Chapter 10

Page 106

1. College Placement Council, Inc., *College Placement Annual* (Bethlehem, Penn.: College Placement Council, Inc., 1984).

Page 111

2. Moody's Investment Services, Inc., *Moody's Stock Survey* (New York: Moody's Investment Services, Inc., 1984).

Page 111

3. Standard and Poor's Corp., *Standard Corporation Descriptions* (New York: Standard and Poor's Corp., 1984).

Chapter 11

Page 119

1. Douglas McGregor, *The Human Side of Enterprise* (New York: McGraw-Hill, 1960).

Additional References

Armstrong, Fiona, and Myra Baum. *A Realistic Job Search.* New York: McGraw-Hill, 1980.

Armstrong, Fiona, and others. *The Reality of Work and Promotion.* New York: McGraw-Hill, 1980.

Asta, Patricia, and Linda Bernbach. *Test Your Vocational Aptitude.* New York: Arco, 1976.

Billingsley, Edmond. *Career Planning and Job Hunting for Today's Student: The Non-Job Interview Approach.* Santa Monica, Calif.: Goodyear, 1978.

Bostwick, Burdette E. *How to Find the Job You've Always Wanted.* 2d ed. New York: Wiley, 1980.

Davis, Keith. *Human Behavior at Work.* 6th ed. New York: McGraw-Hill, 1981.

Feingold, S. Norman. *Counseling for Careers in the 1980's.* Garrett Park, Md.: Garrett Park Press, 1979.

Gainer, Harold N., and Sandra L. Stark. *Choice or Chance: A Guide to Career Planning.* New York: McGraw-Hill, 1979.

Ginzberg, Eli. *Good Jobs, Bad Jobs, No Jobs.* Cambridge, Mass.: Harvard University Press, 1979.

Harkness, Charles A. *Career Counseling: Dreams and Reality.* Springfield, Ill.: C.C. Thomas, 1976.

Healy, Charles C. *Career Development: Counseling Through the Life Stages.* Boston, Mass.: Allyn & Bacon, 1982.

Hilton, Thomas L. *Confronting the Future: A Conceptual Framework for Secondary School Career Guidance.* New York: College Board, 1979.

Holland, John L. *Making Vocational Choices: A Theory of Careers.* Englewood Cliffs, N. J.: Prentice-Hall, 1973.

Jordann, Jean-Pierre, and Martha B. Hyde. *Vocational Maturity During the High School Years.* Edited by Donald E. Super. New York: Teachers College Press, 1979.

Kanter, Rosabeth M. *Men and Women of the Corporation.* New York: Basic Books, 1979.

Klingner, Donald E., and Anthony J. Davis. *The Job-Seeker's Guide: A Workbook for Improving Your Career Situation.* New York: Human Sciences Press, 1980.

Korman, Abraham K. *Organizational Behavior.* Englewood Cliffs, N. J.: Prentice-Hall, 1977.

Moore, Donna J. *Take Charge of Your Own Career.* 2d ed. Bainbridge Is., Wash.: Moore, 1981.

Morgan, Marilyn A., and others. "Career Development Strategies in Industry: Where We Are and Where We Should Be." *Personnel,* March–April 1979, pp. 13–30.

Osipow, Samuel H. *Theories of Career Development.* 3d ed. Englewood Cliffs, N. J.: Prentice-Hall, 1983.

Pilder, Richard J., and William F. Pilder. *How to Find Your Life's Work: Staying Out of Traps and Taking Control of Your Career.* Englewood Cliffs, N. J.: Prentice-Hall, 1981.

Powell, C. Randall. *Career Planning Today.* Dubuque, Ia.: Kendall-Hunt, 1981.

Rogers, Carl R. *On Becoming a Person.* Boston: Houghton Mifflin, 1961.

Rust, H. Lee. *Jobsearch: The Complete Manual for Job Seekers.* New York: AMACOM, 1979.

Schein, Edgar H. *Career Dynamics: Matching Individual and Organizational Needs.* Reading, Mass.: Addison-Wesley, 1978.

Souerwine, Andrew H. *Career Strategies: Planning for Personal Achievement.* New York: AMACOM, 1978.

Srebalus, David J. *Career Development: Concepts and Procedures.* Monterey, Calif.: Brooks-Cole, 1982.

Tolbert, E.L. *Counseling for Career Development.* 2d ed. Boston: Houghton Mifflin, 1980.

Walker, James W. "Does Career Planning Rock the Boat?" *Human Resources Management,* Spring 1978, pp. 2–7.

Walker, James W., and Thomas G. Gutteridge. *Career Planning Practices.* New York: AMACOM, 1979.

Wanous, John P. "Organizational Entry: From Naive Expectations to Realistic Beliefs." *Journal of Applied Psychology* 61 (1976): 22–29.

Welford, A.T. "Thirty Years of Psychological Research on Age and Work." *Journal of Occupational Psychology* 49 (1976): 129–138.

Index